ONE
HUNDRED
YEARS
OF OLD TESTAMENT
INTERPRETATION

ONE HUNDRED YEARS OF OLD TESTAMENT INTERPRETATION

Ronald E. Clements

The Westminster Press

Philadelphia

PUBLISHED BY THE WESTMINSTER PRESS ®

Philadelphia, Pennsylvania

PRINTED IN THE UNITED STATES OF AMERICA

To
Gillian and Marian

Library of Congress Cataloging in Publication Data

Clements, Ronald Ernest, 1929–
    One hundred years of Old Testament interpretation.

    Includes bibliographical references and index.
    1. Bible. O.T. — Criticism, interpretation,
etc. — History — 19th century. 2. Bible. O.T.
— Criticism, interpretation, etc. — History — 20th
century. I. Title.
BS1160.C56 1976   221.6′6   76-23236
ISBN 0-664-24747-4

Contents

61421

List of Journals and Series

Preface

The following work requires some explanation as to its purpose since it is neither an introduction to the Old Testament in the accepted sense nor a comprehensive history of the ways in which the Old Testament has been interpreted since Wellhausen. It is no more than a sketch of the latter, and to have attempted the larger task would have required a volume much greater in size than I have been able to offer. My aim has been to provide the student and general reader with some picture of the main lines of interpretation which have affected the study of the Old Testament, with a particular emphasis upon questions of methodology. In doing this I have concentrated upon the work of a few scholars whose contributions appear to me to have been particularly significant and interesting in this respect. I have also endeavoured where possible to show some of the inter-connections which relate the work of various scholars to each other. Within each of the chapters which deal with the main sections of the Old Testament canon I have endeavoured to maintain a broadly chronological outline of development.

Two major departments of the study and interpretation of the Old Testament have been almost entirely left out of my treatment. One of these is the linguistic and philological examination of the text and language of the literature and the other is that of Palestinian and Near Eastern archaeology. For these omissions I would wish to venture the following reasons, besides my own lack of competence in these specialized fields. One is that both fields of research affect the entire Old Testament, so that to consider them would have required a separate section in each of my main chapter divisions. The other is that each of these departments of study has grown so enormously in the past century that they properly require separate treatments of their own if they are to be described in a sufficiently meaningful way.

For practical reasons I have kept footnotes to a minimum and references to literature to what is essential for a proper understanding of the chronological perspective. I hope I have provided enough information for the reader to be able to find some further treatments of the main issues that are discussed. That my selection of developments may appear somewhat arbitrary has been unavoidable in order to keep the work within a reasonable length. I have also found it necessary at times to indicate where I think scholars have been wrong, without being able to set out all the reasons for my doing so. Undesirable as this is, it seems to me preferable to making the survey no more than a catalogue which remains neutral in its conclusions. I hope that the reader who is unable to accept my judgements will at least see the point of them.

My indebtedness to other scholars should be apparent throughout the book, although I have avoided so far as I have been able to do so the repetition of discussions and surveys which are readily available in other volumes. It remains for me to express my particular thanks to Dr Cecil Northcott of the Lutterworth Press for his kindness in suggesting that I should write this book.

R. E. Clements
1976

1

Introduction

The years since 1870 have witnessed an immense scholarly involvement in the study and interpretation of the Old Testament, closely matching in effort and range that devoted to the study of the New. Both Christians and Jews, as well as historians and orientalists who have admitted allegiance to neither faith, have been intensively occupied with sifting the documents, searching out relevant parallels, and repeatedly asking how, when, and why this literature came into existence. Since the beginning of the Christian era the Old Testament has been used and read in substantially the same form as that in which it exists today, and its earliest literary sources go back approximately a millennium more.

The reasons which led to the quest for a fresh critical understanding of the origins and significance of the Old Testament are certainly to be traced to the years before 1870, and most of the methods and tools of literary and historical scholarship had already become available, and had been tested, by this time. In fact many of the conclusions about the structure and origin of the Old Testament which broke so disturbingly upon the Church and the world in the next decade through the writings in Germany of such scholars as J. Wellhausen and B. Duhm, were certainly not entirely novel or unprecedented. In a great many respects they represented a refinement and consolidation of views that had been propounded for a number of years. What was new was the strength of the case that was now being eagerly canvassed for a fresh critical account of the historical rise of Israel and its religion, and the clarity with which the case was now presented. It made a warm appeal to a wide circle of competent scholarship who were readily able to examine the evidence on which it was based. In the minds of the leading exponents of this higher criticism, as this study came to be called, it was clearly felt that no one had anything to fear from its new truth. Faith would not be overthrown, but rather strengthened, and given a new and more solid foundation on which to rest. Knowledge of the historical facts about the origin of the Old Testament, and the Israelite religion from which it had emerged, would provide a sure foundation upon which faith could build.

Hence in the writings of the new generation of critical scholars there is to be found an evangelical fervour about the manner with which the new insights were publicized and presented. Where breaks were sharply made with traditional Christian and Jewish views about the Old Testament there was felt to be a welcome deliverance from hampering bonds and new and more lasting ties made with truth, morality and piety in a broad human setting. Where the older Christian view of the Old Testament as a book of ancient prophecies about the coming of Jesus Christ was being set aside, it was felt that it was nevertheless being replaced by a fresh and more scholarly apologetic which showed that in the Old Testament were to be found the moral and spiritual foundations of a universal religion. This found in Jesus Christ the fullest embodiment of its own earnestness.

As far as Great Britain was concerned this new religious enthusiasm for the critical approach to the Old Testament is well illustrated in the writings of W. Robertson Smith. His two popular series of lectures, subsequently published as *The Old Testament in the Jewish Church*[1] and *The Prophets of Israel*[2], represent a determined attempt to spread abroad to the widest Christian readership the insights of the new scholarship. Far from regarding this as a threat to the Christian faith, W. Robertson Smith firmly claimed that it brought to this faith a new intellectual foundation. That the Church was not ready for this may be readily conceded and is amply shown by the heresy trials to which Smith was subjected. Nevertheless the achievement of critical scholarship in the interpretation of the Old Testament was immense, so that by the turn of the century virtually all the major centres of theological learning in Europe had embraced its methods and its basic conclusions. Only in America was the reaction to it more intense and more prolonged, where the dismissal of C. H. Toy from his professorship at the Southern Baptist Seminary in 1879[3] reflected a more deep-seated suspicion of critical biblical scholarship and a marked difference in the structure and background of American theological education.

In recent years it has frequently been widely claimed that a cloud of suspicion and error hangs over the pioneers of the newer criticism of the Old Testament on account of their particular theological and philosophical presuppositions. Most especially the purported Hegelianism of Wellhausen has been alleged to constitute a serious weakness, and to show that the fundamental assumptions of this intellectual enterprise were mistaken. Such a claim can only be maintained by substantially disregarding the facts, and by looking away from the actual evidence adduced by these scholars in support of their views. This is not to say, of course, that they were altogether without presuppositions, which would undoubtedly have required that they should have ceased to be children of their own time. A. Kuenen, the distinguished Dutch scholar whose work on the history of Israelite religion stands out as a major achievement of pioneering critical work on the Old Testament,[4] displays a note of rationalism which cannot be entirely denied. So also W. Robertson Smith's attraction to Kuenen's work lends to his own writings something of the same colour. Furthermore we cannot deny features in Wellhausen's assessment of Israel's religion which betray touches of philosophical idealism reminiscent of Hegel. That Wellhausen was drawn to the earlier work of Wilhelm Vatke on Old Testament theology, which was quite markedly Hegelian in its views, is also not to be denied.[5] Yet all these factors in no way amount to an overall demonstration that the rise of critical Old Testament scholarship was the product of a number of contemporary philosophical presuppositions. The essential basis of critical study and its major conclusions were arrived at and upheld by scholars of very varying philosophical, theological and ecclesiastical backgrounds. The underlying conviction of their endeavours was a foundation of common truth which all could reach and share.

If we can single out any one assumption which lies behind the rise and triumph of the critical approach to the Old Testament, it is that a foundation of historical fact can be attained by use of the appropriate methods of study, and that this historical foundation, when known, can shed light upon the true nature of biblical faith. Thus it is readily apparent that the main intention which motivated the newer scholarship was that of reaching something which could be called historical truth, in the conviction that this was itself of intense religious worth. Whilst it is true that there were figures involved in the newer research who felt that their earlier faith was slipping from them, be it Lutheran, Reformed, Catholic or whatever, for the most part it is evident that the critical ap-

3

proach was embraced as an instrument of faith. It was held that it could help to lay bare the truth of God's revelation to his ancient people.

Moreover, it would be wrong to ignore the relationship between the emergence of this new critical approach to the literature of the Old Testament and the much wider intellectual concern with the historical studies and historical methods which arose in the nineteenth century. Methods which had proved successful and illuminating in the study of the classical antiquity of Greece and Rome were clearly also relevant to early Israelite history. Similarly the emergence of whole new areas of knowledge with the rediscovery through archaeology of the ancient civilizations of Egypt and Mesopotamia were of direct concern to the study of the Old Testament. A whole new science of historical research with completely fresh material evidence was being brought to light which made it possible to obtain a knowledge of periods of man's past which had long since been forgotten.

Certainly it is significant that the primary goal of the new scholarship was a historical one, concerned with the recovery of a knowledge of the history of ancient Israel and its religion. In retrospect we can see that this was in fact almost entirely taken up with the latter and that only after the main positions of Old Testament criticism had established themselves were questions concerning Israel's political, social and cultural history brought more fully into the debate. That they have a very considerable bearing on more directly religious issues has become increasingly evident as scholarship has progressed. In consequence the development of scholarship since 1870 has seen a growing diversification of disciplines, with separate subjects coming to enjoy a relative importance of their own. As a result we have been presented with a situation in which a number of basic subjects related to the Old Testament have come to acquire special places within its general interpretation. The history of Israel, the development of its religion, the growth of the Old Testament literature and the theology of the Old Testament have all become basic subjects which are related in separate ways to the interpretation of the Old Testament. No single one of them can claim exclusively to be the only valid way of interpreting the Old Testament, yet each of them owes a great deal to the rise and achievements of critical biblical scholarship since 1870. Each of these subjects occupies an accepted place in theological studies which reflects both the degree to which they are all interrelated, and the difficulty of setting apart any one of them as dispensable, or unable to contribute to the better understanding of the others. While the theology of the Old Testament most naturally reflects the interests of the largest number of those who are occupied with this literature, it is impossible in practice to present such a theology without some basis of attention to literary and historical questions. It is not surprising therefore that we can discern a continual process of interaction taking place between them. When making any survey of research over the period, it is evident that there have been fluctuations of interest, such as for example between the concern with the history of Israelite religion, and that with the theology of the Old Testament.

The story of scholarly endeavour which we can now look back upon, and which can with justification be seen to have established a special place for itself in the wake of the achievements of Wellhausen, is an unfinished one. Many of the most pressing questions are still not easily capable of solution, and for some periods of Israelite history the efforts to establish a detailed scientific chronology have remained beset with uncertainties. The uninitiated reader may at times feel somewhat bewildered by the wide disagreements between scholars which still exist. For example historical questions concerning the Hebrew patriarchs continue to receive widely differing answers from different scholars. No doubt too the theologian may feel at times that his own particular questions addressed to the Old Testament have sometimes been neglected, and that historical, rather than theological, interests have dominated its interpretation. If at times this has been the case, it is scarcely so today, and the large number of books dealing with the theology of the Old Testament shows that this area has attracted renewed interest. In looking at the picture as a whole the reader cannot but become aware that this literature has provided for many a window onto a world that is too little known in our modern times.

Apart from some brief acquaintance with the classical antiquity of Greece and Rome, and a justifiable admiration for the artistic and technological achievements of ancient Egypt, the pre-Christian centuries have often appeared to modern man to be obscure, and of academic rather than practical concern. This is no doubt partly a consequence of the complacent myth of modernity that still beclouds our times, and which regards the past as curious rather than relevant. A familiarity with the Old Testament writings may, along with the evidence now exhibited in abundance in our museums of the splendours of the ancient Egyptian and Mesopotamian worlds, reveal the great depths of insight and heights of aspiration which man attained in his pre-Christian centuries. The researches of archaeologists and ancient historians in the past century have pushed back the frontiers of historical knowledge to a remarkable extent, and have shown how far back the dawn of civilization is set. At times historians of Israel's religion have mistakenly pictured its origins as lying in a primitive world of animism and taboo, of greater interest to the social anthropologist than the theologian. Such an understanding has been seriously in error, and it is to be hoped that the study of the way in which scholars have sought to make clear the background and message of the Old Testament will show why this is so.

---

1. W. Robertson Smith, *The Old Testament in the Jewish Church*, London, 1881. Several reprints were made before a second edition appeared in 1908.
2. W. Robertson Smith, *The Prophets of Israel*, London, 1882; second edition 1895.
3. Toy's dismissal is discussed by J. Clayton, 'Crawford Howell Toy of Virginia', in *The Baptist Quarterly* 24 (1971), pp. 49–57.
4. Especially A. Kuenen, *De Godsdienst van Israel*, Haarlem, 1869. An English translation of this by A. Heath was published in three volumes as *The Religion of Israel*, 1874–5. His work on the Hexateuch was also of significance for the work of Wellhausen, and an English translation by P. H. Wicksteed of a work entitled *The Hexateuch* also appeared (London, 1886). This was a translation of the first part of the second edition of *Historisch-kritisch Onderzoek naar het onstaan en de verzameling van de Boeken des Ouden Verbonds* (First edition three volumes, Leiden,1861–65. The first part only of the second edition appeared in 1885.)
5. The question of the relationship between the work of the two scholars has been examined fully by L. Perlitt, *Vatke und Wellhausen*, BZAW 94, Berlin, 1965. Perlitt concludes that Wellhausen cannot be regarded as having based his views of Israel's history upon the earlier reconstruction of its religious development by Vatke. Vatke's book, *Die Religion des Alten Testaments, I*, appeared in 1835.

2

Interpreting the Pentateuch

Julius Wellhausen was born in Hamelin in 1844 as the son of a Protestant pastor. In 1862 he went to Göttingen to study theology with the intention of entering the ministry of the Church like his father. However, his love of German studies, and his disenchantment with theology, brought him to the point of deciding to abandon that subject. Before doing so, however, a friend sought to interest him in the work of the Tübingen school of research into Christian origins, led by F. C. Baur, and this for a time engaged his interest. The young Wellhausen eventually also found this too speculative to be satisfying, and so he discarded it. At this time the distinguished theologian A. Ritschl was lecturing in Göttingen and Wellhausen formed a warm personal friendship with him, even though he claimed not to understand his theology.

A major turning point in Wellhausen's career came in 1863 when by chance he came to read the *Geschichte des Volkes Israel*,[1] of the great Göttingen Semitist Heinrich Ewald (1803–75). This immediately won his interest and claimed his enthusiasm so that he turned to the study of Hebrew and Semitic languages under Ewald in Göttingen. In the summer of 1870 he received his Licentiate, and for the next two years he taught as a private lecturer there. In 1871 he published his first book devoted to a study of the text of 1 and 2 Samuel,[2] which is of significance for its relevance to Wellhausen's subsequent concern with the sources and structure of the Pentateuch. In 1872, at the age of 28, Wellhausen was called to a professorship of theology in Greifswald, where in 1878, he published his important pioneering work *Geschichte Israels, I.*[3] The storm of controversy which ensued from this took Wellhausen by surprise, and made him into an object of attack from the authorities of the Church. Under the intensity of this opposition, and conscious of the fact that, if he were to remain true to his own insights he could not offer the kind of teaching which theological students wished to receive in order to prepare themselves for the ministry of the Church, Wellhausen resigned in 1882.[4]

For the next three years he taught Semitic languages as a private lecturer in Halle, leaving for Marburg in 1885 to take up a professorship in this subject. His reputation as one who challenged the accepted traditions of the Church followed him here to the extent that he was expressly forbidden to teach the Old Testament. In 1892 he returned to Göttingen to succeed P. de Lagarde as Professor of Semitic Languages. Much of his research in these later years was devoted to the origins of Islam, although he also turned his attention to the problems of the Synoptic Gospels and continued to present in varying publications and new editions of his major works, his conclusions regarding Israelite-Jewish history in the Old Testament period.[5] His death occurred early in 1918.[6]

In his studies Wellhausen set out first and foremost to be a historian, with which he combined in a remarkably adept way the skills of a linguist, literary critic and historian necessary for his task. The most important feature of his study of 1878 was its clarification of the history of Israel's religious institutions, and the consequences that this had for a proper recognition of the sources and structure of the Pentateuch. The fact that the latter was a work composed from sources emanating from different ages had become gradually accepted since the suggestions made in this direction by the Paris doctor Jean Astruc (1684–1766) and the French Catholic priest Richard Simon (1638–1712). Over the years such a view had come to command more and more scholarly support and to rest upon more and more refined and reliable criteria of analysis. Many key insights had been obtained, and, although for a brief period scholars had flirted with theories of the progressive supplementation of an original source document, or of a great miscellany of fragmentary sources, views had increasingly settled upon a recognition of four basic literary source documents, labelled for convenience E^1, E^2, J and D.

Since the work of W. M. L. de Wette (1780–1849) the D source, which comprised a large part of our present book of Deuteronomy, had been identified as the law book which figured in the great reform under King Josiah recorded in 2 Kings 22–23. Thus a fixed anchorage had been found for one source, which should have facilitated the relative placing of the others in the history of the formation of the Pentateuch. Yet this had not proved to be an easy undertaking since, unlike D, none of the others could be readily, or demonstrably, linked with known major events of Israel's history. Even more disconcertingly the relative ordering of the other sources among themselves had not been satisfactorily worked out in a way which could command wide support. The main reason for this was the problem of the two Elohist sources, E^1 and E^2, the first of which clearly provides the basic framework of the completed Pentateuch which we now have.

Scholars had tended to regard the E^1 source as the oldest and most fundamental of the Pentateuchal sources, although others claimed that it was late and not early. Among the latter advocates were the Frenchman Eduard Reuss (1804–91), a vigorous and stimulating teacher, who taught first at the seminary, and later the university, of Strasbourg, and his pupil K. H. Graf. Graf was a strange, and almost eccentric figure, given to ambitious plans and unpopular views, who regretted that he had lost his childhood faith, and who retained an intense interest in Old Testament studies. Throughout his life he remained a schoolteacher, and never obtained a theological professorship. He set out in print the view, which he had learnt in lectures from E. Reuss, that the First Elohist, E^1, which basically corresponds with what scholars have now come to know as the Priestly Document, P, was the latest and not the earliest of the Pentateuchal sources.[7] This was based in the claim that the vast complex of regulations for the ceremonial laws and rituals of Israel's worship which it contained were late and post-exilic. Thus, instead of this compendium of laws preceding the prophets and the early writers of Israel's history, it followed after them, and throughout presupposed them. The law was later than the prophets, which was the antithesis of the view established by Jewish tradition, which had not previously been seriously challenged.

Wellhausen tells that, when he heard of Graf's conclusion, in a private conversation with Albrecht Ritschl, he sensed immediately that it was right, even though he could not at the time examine Graf's reasons.[8] Already in his studies of the books of Samuel and Kings, Wellhausen had come to see that these historical writings did not presuppose a knowledge of the elaborate priestly laws of the First Elohist, which Wellhausen labelled Q but which is now universally recognized as P. Thus he was ready to accept the rightness of Graf's conclusion and to provide it with a basis of scholarly evidence and support which neither Reuss nor Graf had been able to give it. He did this in two main works,

9

the first a series of critical studies of the source analysis of the Hexateuch which were for the most part originally published in the *Jahrbücher für Deutsche Theologie* in the years 1876–77 in which he examined section by section the narratives of the Hexateuch from Genesis to 2 Samuel.[9] The second was his *Geschichte Israels I* of 1878, which was subsequently revised and reprinted as *Prolegomena zur Geschichte Israels*. The first of these works was in every way a necessary preparation for the second. In it Wellhausen followed earlier critics in using criteria of vocabulary usage, characteristics of style, prevalent theological ideas and local colouring in order to distinguish between the various source documents used.

Many of the conclusions arrived at were in line with those of earlier Old Testament scholars, although Wellhausen's own skill as a linguist and his literary sensitivity enabled him to establish his positions with great thoroughness and care. The results of the critical source analysis were used in the *Prolegomena* to present a wide-ranging conspectus of the history of the development of Israel's religious institutions. What was especially original in this picture was the argument that the great collections of cultic and ceremonial laws were late, and that the document in which he believed they were set (Q, now generally called P) was the latest of the Hexateuchal sources. This enabled Wellhausen to provide a coherent and well-founded chronology of the growth of the Hexateuch as a foundation for a proper understanding of the entire literary history of the Old Testament.

As an interpretation of the development of Israel's religious history, this work was an outstanding achievement, even though it only partly fulfilled the promise of its title, since it gave only limited attention to the story of Israel's political and cultural history. Its central concern was the history of Israel's religious institutions of priesthood, temple and sacrifice, and this was brilliantly carried through with great attention to detail. It represented an uncompromising substantiation of Graf's hypothesis, set out with a skill which Graf could not have begun to emulate. The resulting picture of Israel's religious development meant that the documentary source hypothesis as an explanation of the origin of the Hexateuch was lifted onto the plane of religious history. Its fundamental conclusions reached beyond the minute details of verbal and literary comparisons. Those who criticized it as being too refined, and who challenged the validity of analysing short passages, and even individual verses, into strata from separate sources, could make little impact on the generally convincing nature of its overall presentation. To

10

challenge this required the putting forward of a credible alternative.

In this broad critical picture of Israel's religious history the understanding of the origin and structure of the Pentateuch, or the Hexateuch as Wellhausen argued, provided the central subject. The question that was most at issue was that of the date of the ceremonial law, with its underlying assumption that Israel was a priestly theocracy. Wellhausen showed that, on the evidence of the Old Testament witness to Israel's life during the period of the monarchy, the nation had not functioned at that time as such a priestly theocracy. On the contrary this theocracy was an ideal, a pattern fastened onto a picture of the past. The more reliable evidence of the nation's beginnings in the books of Judges and Samuel showed a much more primitive organization, and confirmed the view that the idea of a Jewish theocracy, centred upon a law given to Moses, was a post-exilic creation which had only arisen once Israel had lost its own national existence. The real source of the people's religious spirit was not to be found in an ancient lawgiver, but in the prophets, who, in the years before the nation's fall, had established a truly ethical faith in one God.

In all his writings Wellhausen was supremely a historian, albeit a religious historian. His task was to understand, evaluate and use the sources available in order to present a picture of Israel's history in the Old Testament period as it actually had been. When later he turned his attention to the origins of Islam the same passionate historical concern was evident. So far as the Old Testament was concerned it is significant that Wellhausen did not involve himself with other questions relating to it, but re-presented his main conclusions regarding the history in a number of separate publications, as well as in further editions of the *Prolegomena*. Even so the reader can readily discern behind this historical passion a deep religious feeling, and a very real sensitivity to theological issues. He did not hesitate to see the crowning glory of the religion of the Old Testament in the preaching of Jesus, nor did he shrink from expressing his own sympathies and antipathies in discussing the rise of the Jewish sectarian parties.[10] W. Robertson Smith, who more prominently than any other sought to spread throughout Britain the methods, aims and conclusions of the higher criticism, presents a strong apologetic for it in his preface to the English translation of the *Prolegomena*: 'the main reason why so many parts of the Old Testament are practically a sealed book even to thoughtful people is simply that they have not the historical key to the interpretation of that wonderful literature'.[11] Wellhausen himself would surely have agreed.

In understanding his historical task Wellhausen rightly saw the central problem to lie in the interpretation of the Hexateuch, since it was here that the greatest differences emerged between the traditional date ascribed to the origin of its contents, as a uniform whole, and that which literary criticism had brought to light. Only when this had been clarified and explained, and the proper sequence of the sources established, could a coherent picture be drawn which made adequate sense of evidence preserved elsewhere in the Old Testament. The objection has sometimes been raised against Wellhausen's reconstruction of Israel's history that it leans heavily upon a Hegelian philosophy, which has made it too rigorously evolutionary in its presentation of history. The fact that Hegelian ideas can be traced in Wellhausen's work is not to be denied, but they certainly did not determine his general method and approach. If there is any one underlying assumption that runs through all his work it is that the uncovering of the truth about Israel's history is itself an achievement of immense religious and spiritual worth.

For Wellhausen, the interpretation of the Hexateuch, when understood critically, provided a key to the understanding of the whole development of Israel's religion. Nevertheless it offered, in his estimation, only a very limited guide towards a knowledge of the real beginnings of Israel in the days of Moses and the patriarchs. In his scheme even the earliest of the Hexateuchal sources had not been composed before the middle of the ninth century BC, and so it could tell us nothing of the nature of the oldest religion of Israel. Rather, as Wellhausen believed, it reflected the situation that had developed by the time of its composition. It was this conclusion that was challenged, and replaced by a more convincing alternative, in the work of Hermann Gunkel (1862–1932).[12]

Gunkel's great contribution to the interpretation of the Old Testament lay in a remarkably new awareness of the place and function of literature in early societies. To an unusual degree he was sensitive to the aesthetic and spiritual potentialities of literature, and used this to uncover from the Old Testament writings a picture of the spiritual life and ideals of early Israel. He is rightly regarded as the pioneer of *form* criticism as a method of biblical study, even though the *type* criticism (German *Gattungsgeschichte*) which he introduced reached far beyond questions of literary form alone. He himself began as a New Testament scholar, and became the teacher of both M. Dibelius and R. Bultmann, who were able to carry over into the study of the New Testament methods which Gunkel had first established with regard to the Old. In his type criticism we can find the essential insights which lie behind the methods of form criticism, traditio-historical criticism and redaction criticism.

Like Wellhausen, Gunkel was the son of a Lutheran pastor, and he was born in Springe, near Hannover in 1862. He started out his theological studies with research in the New Testament but then changed to the Old, where his first major published work was entitled *Schöpfung und Chaos in Urzeit und Endzeit* (*Creation and Chaos at the Beginning and End of Time*).[13] In it he examined the problem of apocalyptic in its relationship to ancient Near Eastern mythology, and argued very strongly that the influence of this mythology was to be seen in both Jewish and Christian apocalyptic writings. Thus at this early stage Gunkel expressed his deep conviction that the Bible could be shown to have received deep influences from the surrounding peoples of the ancient East, a claim which immediately drew forth the sharp criticism of Wellhausen against him.[14]

This interest in the background of the Bible led Gunkel to associate himself with what was to become known as the History of Religion School. Gunkel's views of the Bible differed sharply from the way in which some members of that school ultimately carried their conclusions, making the entire New Testament little more than a late reflection of ancient myths.[15] What mattered deeply to him was the awareness that there was a continuity between what we find in the religion of the Old Testament and that which was just beginning to be rediscovered of the religious life of Mesopotamia and ancient Egypt. We could not therefore be satisfied with the presentation of Israel's religious history which Wellhausen had put forward, which left out of account any significant influence from outside.

In the years before the First World War the study of the connections between the Bible and the rediscovered religions of Mesopotamia became known as the Bible–Babel controversy and was brought under the deepest suspicion. This was a sharply conducted academic debate over the question of traces of Babylonian religion and mythology in the Old Testament which began with a lecture given in 1902 by Friedrich Delitzsch before the German Oriental Society in Berlin in the presence of the Kaiser. The effect was to draw suspicion upon all who, like Gunkel, were interested in exploring the Old Testament in the light of what could be learnt of its background in the ancient world. Since Gunkel, having turned from the study of the New Testament to the Old, was already looked at askance by some other Old Testament scholars on the grounds that he had not had a full training in Semitic languages, his association with an unpopular cause was a serious disadvantage in the highly competitive theological scene which prevailed in Germany before the war. It is not surprising therefore to discover that Gunkel was not well received by many of his fellow biblical scholars, and that he was compelled to wait an inordinately long time in order to obtain an ordinary professorship. This did not finally occur until he was called to Giessen in 1907, when he had already published a number of outstanding works of scholarship.

In the prevailing dominance of Wellhausen's views in Old Testament circles, it was only slowly that the real genius that was present in Gunkel's studies came to be realized, and many of his insights only received their full and rightful recognition very late in his career. Only in his last years as a teacher was his true greatness honoured in Germany, when increasingly the wide relevance of suggestions and analyses which he had originally published long before came to be realized. In some respects the full exploration of paths which he pioneered has still to be completed.

Gunkel's early work on apocalyptic drew forth criticism from Wellhausen on this question of method, and led to a tendency on the part of the two scholars to speak as if they were more greatly at variance with each other's work than was in fact the case. In its main features Gunkel's work fully presupposed that of Wellhausen, and built substantially upon it. Where the work differed was in its understanding of the nature of the major documentary sources of the Pentateuch. For Wellhausen we have seen that these were regarded as original compositions made at particular periods in Israel's history, and therefore strongly reflecting the life of these periods. Gunkel however had come to see that their composition was only a relatively late phase in the history of the material which they contained, and that this material must at one time have existed separately as oral tradition. Not only so, but the present setting of the various narratives and regulations as part of a continuous history must have been preceded by an earlier stage when they were independently related to particular places and customs. This was their original setting in life (German *Sitz im Leben*), which was important for an understanding of many of the features retained in them. By examining the narratives and laws separately, as individual units, Gunkel believed that it was possible to recover a knowledge of a much earlier period of Israel's life than that in which the final composition of the source documents had taken place. Thus whereas Wellhausen's brilliant source criticism had brought to light four main layers, or stages, in the growth of the Hexateuch, each with its own reflection of Israel's religious institutions, Gunkel was able to carry this much further into obtaining a picture of greater depth than Wellhausen had achieved.

This major advance in Pentateuchal studies, which represents the establishing of new methods of form, and traditio-historical, criticism, was introduced by Gunkel into his commentary on the book of Genesis, which was first published in 1901.[16] The introduction to this was translated into English and published as *The Legends of Genesis*.[17] In it Gunkel applied his insights to the stories of the Hebrew patriarchs and showed that we could obtain from these narratives a most illuminating picture of the earliest stage of Israelite spirituality and piety.

Behind this study by Gunkel was a whole new understanding of the place of literature in early societies, and especially of the way in which such early literature reflected its close connection with oral story telling and tradition. Thus, as Gunkel saw it, each type of narrative had a particular place, or function, in society, so that we should not regard such stories as free, and arbitrarily chosen compositions. Rather they conformed to certain basic patterns which were determined by the particular uses to which such stories were put. Thus for example, it was possible to see that several of the stories about the Hebrew patriarchs had been designed to explain how certain places had become sanctuaries. Others explained why certain customs were to be performed, or endeavoured to explain how peculiar geographical features had arisen. Subsequently these separate stories had been put together to form chains of stories relating to particular persons, or regions. Eventually they had been built up into the extended sources which Wellhausen's documentary hypothesis had done so much to clarify.

Gunkel worked on the assumption that it was these separate stories, taken and interpreted individually, which offered the most significant and fascinating feature of the book of Genesis. Each story had been composed in a specific, and very ancient, setting, and so it was in relation to this that its fullest meaning became apparent. By paying regard to such stories it was possible, Gunkel saw, to penetrate into the earliest spiritual life of Israel, and to probe its aims, ideals and practices. It provided a key to recovering invaluable insights into the earliest pre-prophetic faith and practice of Israel. This antedated by centuries the period when the earliest of the documentary sources of J and E had been composed. In a striking way also such material provided evidence of the truly popular character of the Old Testament, in contrast to the more widely affirmed emphasis upon its great individual heroes of faith, especially the prophets. It was evident to Gunkel that such narratives which have been preserved in Genesis bear a relationship to other early popular folk-tales and legends of many nations, and he drew attention to such comparative materials in later editions of his commentary. Yet there is no evidence that Gunkel consciously arrived at his conclusions regarding the Old Testament by carrying over conclusions reached in other fields of folk literature.[18]

In line with his work on apocalyptic, Gunkel was, however, very conscious of the importance of examining and comparing the literary and religious background of Israel's neighbours. This was becoming more and more possible through the continuing discoveries of ancient text materials from Mesopotamia and Egypt. For Gunkel these were not looked upon as the source of biblical ideas, but rather as the background of thought and custom which illustrated what we find in the Old Testament. To deny the relationship of the religion of ancient Israel to those of its neighbours would have been, for Gunkel, a denial of the real historical context in which the Bible had arisen.

The method of *Gattungsgeschichte* which Gunkel had initiated was capable of being applied over a wide area of the writings of the Old Testament. Although Gunkel himself dealt initially with its use in the interpretation of the narratives of Genesis, his friend and associate Hugo Gressmann (1877–1927) carried over the method into a very full study of the narrative sections of the book of Exodus:[19] and also, more briefly, into the study of the historical books from Joshua to 2 Kings.[20] We shall have occasion to consider the latter work later, so that the former study is our more immediate concern. In it Gressmann sought to show the character of the narratives about Moses and the Israelite exodus from Egypt, with a concern to demonstrate their particular quality as Israelite saga.

Even more than Gunkel, Gressmann laid emphasis upon the connections which were to be traced between the stories of the book of Exodus and other ancient legends and sagas. The approach is throughout that of traditio-history, examining the individual units to learn from them their original setting and purpose. At the same time Gressmann was not indifferent to seeking to look beneath the present form of the material to find out from it what had actually happened to Israel in Egypt, and how it had escaped from thence.

The most noticeable immediate impact of the work was to open up a number of rather speculative essays regarding the whole episode, centred upon the suggestion that the original mount Sinai must have been an active volcano, and must therefore be sought, not in the Sinai peninsula but much further east. On a very important question Gressmann challenged Wellhausen's assessment of the literature. This was over the date of the Decalogue of Exodus 20:2–17,[21] which Wellhausen had placed late in Israel's history, but which Gressmann now argued was to be set much earlier since it bore no evidence of the influence of Canaan.[22] He argued that it was older than the prophets, and represented one of the foundational traditions of Israelite religion. On this point he was in agreement with the work of another German scholar, Paul Volz (1871–1941), who used the Decalogue, and the ascription to it of a very early date, as a basis for expounding the work of Moses.[23]

Gressmann's studies were only one example of the way in which the method of *Gattungsgeschichte* enabled scholarship to go behind the source documents which Wellhausen's work had demonstrated. The various narrative parts which were incorporated into the longer documentary sources could be studied by themselves, and their history examined before they had been given a wider literary context. The same was true of the basic law collections, such as the Decalogue, and in fact of almost all the materials which had become part of the Hexateuch.

In consequence, for the next two or three decades we find the interpretation of the Pentateuch being conducted along two paths. The first of these was the further study of the evidence for the four main documents which had become identified with Pentateuchal criticism. The second, and in many respects more fruitful, work lay in the examination of individual parts of the Pentateuch along the lines of Gunkel's method.

In the former category we can note that two of the basic documentary sources, E and D, showed certain peculiar features which especially invited further consideration. Of the first of these the point that was most noticeable was that the passages which were ascribed to it were disjointed, and in some cases fragmentary, so that they did not fit together to make a continuous narrative. In several instances too, narratives from E were duplicates, with some modifications, of narratives that were also to be found in J. Therefore E could not be regarded as a completely independent work. The explanation for this which critics put forward was that E was basically an epic history of the beginnings of Israel which ran parallel in considerable measure to that of J. When a

17

redactor had come to combine the two epic histories together to make one comprehensive story, he had used J as a basis, working parts of E into this, thereby expanding it. This was the view proposed by Otto Procksch,[24] who argued that, in spite of its fragmentary remnants, it had once been a great saga of the origins of Israel written and preserved by the northern tribes. This was not the only possible explanation, however, and P. Volz later argued that E had never been a continuous document, and the attempt to identify it had been mistaken.[25] The material that had been so classed was either such that could not properly be separated from J, or it represented various glosses and additions that had been made to it.

Most scholars, however, have not been willing to set aside E as not being a part of the four source hypotheses in the structure of the Pentateuch. In a rather different direction a further modification of Wellhausen's position was advocated by Otto Eissfeldt (1887–1973) who sought to divide up the J document into an earlier L source and rather later J document.[26] Substantially the same view has been proposed by G. Fohrer, with the variation that the earlier document is described as N.[27]

The D source, which belonged among the group of four main documents, is distinctive because of its compactness, in that it is virtually coterminous with the book of Deuteronomy. It also shows a remarkable homogeneity of style. This is certainly very much more marked than in the case of the other documents, and can in fact readily be noted even in an English translation of the Old Testament. Since the days of de Wette the D law book had been identified with the law book found in the temple in Josiah's time (621 BC). Since there are several points of similarity in language and thought between the E and D sources, C. F. Burney suggested that both of them represent written documents which have emanated from Northern Israel.[28] Thus we are asked to recognize a regional, as well as a chronological separation between the four source documents, which had not been properly allowed for in Wellhausen's scheme of their origin and history.

Such a suggestion was taken up and developed by several scholars quite independently, notably A. C. Welch in Scotland,[29] A. Bentzen in Denmark[30] and G. von Rad in Germany.[31] Both the latter scholars argued that much of the material contained in D had a substantial history reaching back into a quite early period of the history of the northern tribes. In the wake of these studies a large number of further researches have appeared aimed at probing into the sources and traditions which lie behind Deuteronomy. A characteristic feature in all of them has been that they have accepted that it represented a distinctive branch of Israelite tradition.

The P document also has come in for further studies which have, over the years, resulted in a substantially revised estimate of it. The Jewish scholar Y. Kaufmann used a different understanding of P as a lever with which to topple the whole of Wellhausen's picture of the growth of the Pentateuch.[32] This was the most detailed and far reaching work of its kind. Kaufmann sought to find evidence for a pre-exilic date for this material in the accounts of the cultic prescriptions of P. With this as a foundation he argued that P itself, as a written document, must be of pre-exilic origin and represent a stream of tradition which ran parallel to that of D. Thus the entire picture of the development of Israel's religious institutions, which lay at the heart of Wellhausen's reconstruction of Israel's history, was taken to be false. In spite of some support, especially from his fellow Jewish scholars, Kaufmann's view has not proved generally convincing. Much of the reason for this has been due to the fact that traditio-historical research, based on the lines laid down by Gunkel, has come to recognize that all four of the main Pentateuchal sources contain material which is far older than the time at which the final document came to be composed. Kaufmann's arguments therefore, were they to be sustained, do not go beyond establishing the presence of early material in P, without really showing that P itself is of such an early date. Even this conclusion, however, must be set in a different light in view of another marked trend in the criticism of the P source. This has argued increasingly that, in spite of its being labelled P, for Priestly, on account of the extensive range of priestly rules and instructions which it contained, most of these had not originally belonged to it. Rather P must be seen as primarily a historical narrative, into which various collections of priestly instructional material have been incorporated in progressive stages. It is likely in fact that most of the book of Leviticus did not originally stem from the P source, but represents a collection of rules and prescriptions which have been incorporated into it at a later stage.[33] In the case of some of this material it is probable that when this took place P had already been expanded with the earlier Pentateuchal sources of J and E. This, however, is to carry the story of Pentateuchal interpretation far forward beyond the years of work by Gunkel and Gressmann.

We have pointed out that from the time of Gunkel, Pentateuchal criticism was able to move forward along two paths. The first of these was the further examination of the evidence concerning the four main written documentary sources. The other was to pursue the *gattungsgeschichtliche* method which recognized that these four source documents were comprised of collections of narratives and laws which had originally once existed independently as oral tradition. Gunkel's studies of the patriarchal stories of Genesis had thus been able to go behind the J and E sources to recognize that the individual stories about the Hebrew patriarchs had once had a different setting, which had decisively determined their character. Gressmann had worked similarly on the narratives of the book of Exodus, which covered stories from J, E and P. In the hands of these scholars the stage of 'collection' into one of the longer written documents was not regarded as of anything like the significance which Wellhausen had accorded to it. It was clearly possible to extend this insight much further and to examine virtually the entire Pentateuch along these lines. This would not ignore the division of the material between the four main sources, but would concentrate rather on the individual narratives and law collections.

An early worker in this particular field was the Norwegian scholar Sigmund Mowinckel (1884–1966), who had been a pupil of Gunkel's in Giessen before the First World War. After the publication of his commentary on Genesis, Gunkel had turned his attention to the book of Psalms. He recognized that here were certain basic types of psalm, just as there were basic types of folk narrative. It was this aspect of Gunkel's work which had attracted the interest of Mowinckel. He first of all developed Gunkel's method with regard to the prophetic book of Jeremiah and then much more extensively in the Psalter. In the light of these latter studies, however, Mowinckel turned his attention to the Decalogue of Exodus 20:2–17.[34] He argued that an old tradition lay behind the account of Yahweh's revelation at Sinai, and that the Decalogue represented a collection which had grown up over a considerable period of years. But what was its *Sitz im Leben*? Mowinckel drew attention to several elements which betrayed a connection with features of Israelite worship which his studies of the Psalms had led him to ascribe to a great autumnal celebration in the temple in Jerusalem in pre-exilic Israel. This had entitled the Festival of Yahweh's Enthronement.

What was significant here was the claim that a collection of laws as important as that of the Decalogue had originally been formulated in the setting of Israel's cult, and that the narrative context which this collection enjoyed had also taken its shape as a result of its transmission in the cult. This amounted to a substantial modification of the picture of the oral stage of the transmission of Pentateuchal narratives from that put forward by Gunkel. The latter had focused his attention almost entirely upon the popular folk setting of the old narratives, but now this was being extended to include the rites and liturgies of worship as a formative factor in the composition of the stories. Such an idea as this, that we could see behind some of the Pentateuchal narratives the creative influence of the cult, was applicable to other parts of the Pentateuch as well. One section in particular that was quickly brought into the discussion here was the story of the exodus contained in Exodus 1–15. The Danish scholar J. Pedersen suggested that the basic tradition here had originally taken shape as a liturgy for the celebration of Passover.[35] The stage of oral tradition was thereby seen as a period of cultic transmission, when the main structure of the narrative had been established. Pedersen himself used this suggestion as a reason for casting doubt upon the division of the material between three main literary sources, J, E and P, although it would be possible to make such a claim only in regard to the pre-history of J. In spite of enjoying a measure of support, with modifications, from a number of scholars, some decisive objections against Pedersen's view have been made by G. Fohrer.[36]

Working from a rather different direction from Mowinckel, but nonetheless making full use of the insights of form criticism and traditio-history, the German scholar A. Alt (1883–1956) published in 1934 a remarkably fruitful study of the origins of Israelite law.[37] He noted two main forms of law, a basic type of case law, such as we find well represented in the Book of the Covenant of Exodus 20:22–23:19, and a more distinctive form of apodictic law, which is best exemplified in the Decalogue of Exodus 20:2–17. In respect of the latter he argued that its special form as direct speech from God indicated that it had at one time been orally transmitted in the cult, and that such a cultic setting was in any case essential for an understanding of it as law. It was because the deity lay behind the commandment to impose punishment upon offenders that it could rightly be regarded as law. Thus, from a different approach, he had arrived at conclusions which could be compared with those of Mowinckel. This particular understanding of the Decalogue has obtained a wide following, and has tended to encourage still further the view that several features related to the form and early history of material contained in the Pentateuch can best be explained by positing a period of cultic transmission. This setting in a context of worship has been seen as a strong influence upon the structure and literary form of the whole biblical account of God's revelation at Sinai.

On the question of the Decalogue, the notion that it was a distinctive type of law which had originally had its setting in the worship which Israel's ancestors had brought with them from the desert was set in a different light by arguments put forward by G. E. Mendenhall.[38] He drew attention to the fact that stipulations, couched in a similar second person style to that of the apodictic law, were to be found in ancient vassal-treaties, of which several examples were known from the Hittite empire of the late second millenium BC. This led Mendenhall to argue that the Decalogue was formulated on the basis of such a type of vassal-treaty which must have been adapted in Israel, by Moses, to serve a special religious end. Not only so, but the whole tradition of covenant-making in Israel, including the written accounts of the Sinai covenant in the books of Exodus and Deuteronomy, showed traces of the Israelite adaptation of this vassal-treaty form. The debate on this issue still continues, but it is of interest to note it here, since it marks a significant alternative to the various attempts which have been made to trace the original oral stage of parts of the Pentateuchal narrative to a setting in the ancient cult of Israel.

It is not practicable to list here all the wide variety of studies which have been published in an endeavour to uncover as full a picture as possible of the history of the Pentateuchal traditions in their pre-literary stage. Not only have the books of Genesis and Exodus been dealt with in this way, but in various ways almost the entire Pentateuch has been covered by scholars seeking to recover a picture of the history through which the material has passed before being taken up into one or other of the major source documents. All of these studies may quite fairly be regarded as a direct application of the methods of Gunkel to the source criticism which Wellhausen's researches had established as the foundation of studies into Israel's history.

In its consequences for the interpretation of the Pentateuch this method of *Gattungsgeschichte* overturned some of the conclusions of Wellhausen. Most of all it cut loose many of the narratives and rules describing Israel's cultic practice from the chronological scheme which Wellhausen had established from his dating of the documentary sources. The actual history of Israel's religious institutions may not have followed such a clear-cut chronological sequence as Wellhausen's researches had supposed. The Pentateuch in fact revealed a picture of Israel's religious life in greater width and depth than source criticism had originally claimed. Increasingly it was becoming clear that it was a rather narrow and arbitrary position to regard the four main documentary strata as the most significant layers of the Pentateuch for its interpretation. Already Gunkel had written a commentary on Genesis which accepted such source criticism, but which based almost all its interpretative comments upon the much earlier stage of the composition of the independent narrative units. The time was now ripe to consider more fully the consequences of the bringing together of these smaller units into longer written narratives, and even to go beyond this to inquire about the stages by which these sources had been combined together until our present Pentateuch had come into existence.

This brings us very directly to the work of two German scholars, whose researches on the Pentateuch represent the most comprehensive effort to extend the insights of Gunkel still further. These are Gerhard von Rad (1901–71) and Martin Noth (1902–68). G. von Rad was born in Nuremberg and we have already noted that his study of 1929 marked an important step in the inquiry into the traditions which lay behind Deuteronomy, and the particular historical setting which the book as a whole presupposed. He carried his Pentateuchal studies still further in 1933 with an examination of the structure and theology of the P document in which he endeavoured to show that this source was itself composed from two earlier sources which he labelled P[A] and P[B].[39] In 1938 he went on to publish a study entitled *The Form-Critical Problem of the Hexateuch*,[40] which marked pioneer work in the redaction-critical study of the Hexateuch. In this von Rad sought to trace the origin of the framework which the J narrative had given to the individual traditions which he had used, and to show how J had used this older material for a particular purpose of his own. By doing this he went beyond the recognition that each of the smaller narrative units had its own setting in life, and inquired about the setting in life which belonged to J as the first of the longer written sources of the Hexateuch.

In the attempt to unveil the origin of the particular framework of J, von Rad pointed to what he termed short historical credos, most especially in Deuteronomy 6:20–24; 26:5b–9 and Joshua 24:2b–13. Although these were now preserved in later written sources, he argued that they were typical of the kind of brief historical summary, or confession, which had at one time been used as part of a liturgical affirmation of faith in acts of worship. For the original setting of such a confession of God's saving actions he suggested the Feast of Weeks in Gilgal in the early days of Israel's settlement in Canaan. Since the most basic of the summaries did not mention the convenant-making and law-giving on

23

Sinai, von Rad argued that this element of the tradition had been woven into the comprehensive picture at a late stage of its development. What J had done was to take over this basic outline summary of God's actions on Israel's behalf, and to fill it out with all sorts of additional traditions drawn from various tribal and regional sources. The result was that traditions which had at one time been used in the context of the cult were de-sacralized, and connected into a great national epic. Once J had established this basic outline of events it remained the fundamental scheme which had been used in all subsequent presentations of Israel's origins.

The importance of this study by von Rad is very considerable, since it raised new questions with regard to the interpretation of the Pentateuch. In presenting his picture of the sources of the Pentateuch Wellhausen had been concerned to ask what historical weight should be attached to each of them. The question of their origin was viewed mainly in relation to the degree of historical reliability which could be attached to them. Now von Rad was asking a more searching question as to why J had been written at all. What particular religious, or political, situation was being served by its composition? With these questions the interest had shifted away from asking how accurate was Israel's picture of its past, to that of asking what kind of God do people believe in when they present their past in this way.

What von Rad had achieved was a plausible hypothesis about the origins of the writing of epic history in Israel. However, this hypothesis rested upon assumptions about the date and original setting of certain brief summaries of Israel's past, which were admitted to be preserved in documents of a much later time. We cannot be sure that these short 'historical credos' are as old as von Rad's hypothesis requires, nor can we find confirmation that they had originally functioned in the way that he suggested.

In the wake of his study a number of critiques of it have pointed to the fact that it is far more probable that these summaries are of a date which is later than that of J.[41] Instead of their pointing to the outline of events which J had used, they rather point to that which J had established. Even if this is the case, however, as is most likely, the more fundamental questions which are raised in von Rad's study remain unaffected. These concern the setting of J as an epic history, and a recognition of the way in which the literary and religious interests of J as an author have shaped the meaning and interpretation of the materials which he has used. In any case von Rad's essay rightly marks a new development in

24

the study of the history of the redaction of the Pentateuch, and has renewed interest in the four main source documents from a different direction from that which had been uppermost in the interest of Wellhausen.

The work of Martin Noth concerned itself with the whole range of problems relating to the history of the formation of the Pentateuch. From the days of Wellhausen to von Rad it was taken for granted that the main documentary sources extend into the book of Joshua, so that it is more appropriate to speak of Hexateuchal, rather than Pentateuchal, sources. In 1938, however, Martin Noth published a commentary on the book of Joshua which discounted the view that the main J, E and P sources were to be found there at all.[42] There were no clear signs that the narratives and lists of Joshua had ever belonged to any of these sources, and scholars had tended to work on this assumption, rather than to demonstrate it with any assurance.

In carrying this line of research further, Noth published in 1943 a study of the two main historical narrative works outside the Pentateuch, that extending from Joshua to 2 Kings and that comprising 1 and 2 Chronicles, Ezra and Nehemiah.[43] He showed clearly that the book of Joshua could not be properly said to comprise the same documentary sources which are evident in the books from Genesis to Numbers. Since scholars had for a long time been ready to recognize that the book of Deuteronomy stood by itself as composed from a D source, what was left was a Tetrateuch of Genesis to Numbers, which had been composed from the three sources J, E and P. The whole of the material contained in these four books was dealt with extensively by Noth in a study published in 1948 under the title *Überlieferungsgeschichte des Pentateuch (A History of Pentateuchal Traditions)*.[44] In this work Noth offered a brief review of the main problems concerning the J, E and P sources, and then considered very fully the pre-history of the material contained in them. The work represents the fullest exploration of the traditio-historical method in regard to the four books from Genesis to Numbers.

Whilst accepting the main conclusions which von Rad had published, Noth went further in seeking to understand how the material had passed through progressive stages from originally existing as short narrative units and lists to becoming larger narrative complexes and eventually forming part of a great national history. In this process he argued for the importance of five great themes which had served as magnets to draw the various smaller traditions together. These were:

the promise to the patriarchs, the exodus from Egypt, the wandering in the wilderness, the revelation at Sinai and the entry into the land. By means of these themes it had been possible to include an immense variety of material under a basic interpretative motif which gave it a particular place in the overall scheme of the Tetrateuchal history.

Noth's work marks a most interesting phase of Pentateuchal study. It is a fresh endeavour to assess the historical importance of the documentary sources, and their underlying traditions, in the light of Gunkel's recognition that a substantial dimension of historical depth lies behind each of them. The fact that it poses special problems and calls for the re-examination of certain questions must also be accepted. To pursue these would, however, carry us far beyond the scope of this survey of the main lines of interpretation.

In all the work that we have reviewed the importance of Wellhausen's original source analysis remains unchallenged. It required nevertheless to be supplemented by techniques of form, and traditio-historical, study which Gunkel introduced. From time to time, however, some scholars have sought to use the so-called traditio-historical method in an attempt to challenge the very foundations of the Wellhausian source criticism. We have already noted how J. Pedersen tried to do this with regard to the material of Exodus 1–15 by arguing that it represented a collection of traditions which had originally taken shape in a Passover liturgy. Other, even more conservative, views have from time to time been put forward, usually by seeking to deny the validity of the methods and evidence which Wellhausen had used.

We may note, however, that the Swedish scholar I. Engnell (1907–64) argued against Wellhausen's source criticism on the basis of what he termed a thoroughgoing application of traditio-historical method.[45] In this he allied himself with the conclusion of Martin Noth that we must start from the recognition that we are concerned with the Tetrateuch of Genesis to Numbers, since Deuteronomy must be regarded as part of a separate work. The Tetrateuch, therefore was labelled by Engnell as the P work, whilst Deuteronomy was part of the separate D work which stretched from Deuteronomy to 2 Kings. Each of these works, Engnell argued, contained a great deal of old material. So far as Genesis to Numbers is concerned, he maintained that this contains both old pre-exilic material and other material of post-exilic date. We must not, however, seek to apportion these materials out between separate documentary sources since these never existed as such. Engnell maintained that the transmission had been oral until the time it had been

26

redacted by P to form the P work.

This was to introduce two rather arbitrary assertions. The first was that no extended written sources had been used in the composition of Genesis to Numbers, and the second was that P was not to be understood as the author of one of the Tetrateuchal sources, but as the final redactor of the whole. This latter point was asserted, rather than demonstrated, by Engnell, and it identified P with what other scholars were terming R^{JEP}, that is the redactor of the combined JEP sources. This was simply adding confusion to the problem, since it was not difficult to see why earlier scholars had wished to make a clear distinction between the later, P, and the earlier, JE, source material in Genesis to Numbers.[46]

It is also noteworthy that Engnell understood the idea of a Tetrateuch quite differently from Noth, even though he claimed to be basing his presentation on that by the German scholar. Whereas Noth argued that J had at one time continued his story to tell of the occupation of the land, and dealt at some length to show that P had not done so, Engnell simply ignored the question of whether any of the material in the Tetrateuch pointed beyond the end of the book of Numbers. To do this was to ignore some of the most complex, yet significant, issues in Pentateuchal research.

Overall therefore it may be argued that the attempt to replace a basic documentary source criticism by resort to some alternative explanation for the evident fact that the Pentateuch contains material of different ages has not been a success. Certainly it is a mistake to regard literary criticism and traditio-historical criticism as alternatives to each other. In reality the one builds on the other, and disregard of this fact leads to confusion rather than clarity in seeking to understand how the Pentateuch has come into being. To discount the main documentary sources, which have for so long been central to Pentateuchal criticism, is to set aside evidence of some of the most important stages of its composition. However it may certainly be admitted that it would also be a false emphasis to regard the stages represented by these sources as the only important ones in the growth of the Pentateuch. What we have in this great collection of history and laws is a complex structure built up of many strata. If the interpretation of the whole is to be comprehensive it must take proper account of each of these.

It is fitting to close this survey with a recollection of the important part that Pentateuchal criticism has played in Old Testament research. Not only is the Pentateuch the first division of the Old Testament canon, but it is also the one which covers the greatest span of years. The gap between the dates of its oldest and latest material is approximately a millennium, which represents an immense period in a nation's history. No adequate picture can be gained of the actual course of Israel's history, nor the origins of its religion, without some workable conclusions about the date and structure of the Pentateuch. To interpret this work therefore is to become involved in some of the most central questions which the Old Testament poses.

---

1. Translated into English by R. Martineau as *The History of Israel*, in seven volumes (fourth edition, London, 1883).
2. J. Wellhausen, *Der Text der Bücher Samuelis*, Göttingen, 1871.
3. J. Wellhausen, *Geschichte Israels, I,* Marburg, 1878; second edition, *Prolegomena zur Geschichte Israels*, 1883. An English translation of this second edition by J. S. Black and A. Menzies entitled *Prolegomena to the History of Israel* was published in 1885. A reprint of this with a further change of title to *Prolegomena to the History of Ancient Israel* was made in 1957 (Harper Torch-books, New York).
4. An extract from Wellhausen's letter of resignation is given by W. Zimmerli, *The Law and the Prophets*, Oxford, 1965, p. 22.
5. These especially included, *Israelitische und Jüdische Geschichte*, Berlin, 1894, and the article 'Israel' in the *Encyclopaedia Britannica*, 1881, which was reprinted as an appendix to the English translation of the *Prolegomena* in 1885, and further published separately in 1891. The original German text of this was originally circulated privately by Wellhausen to his friends and finally published in *Grundrisse zum Alten Testament* edited by R. Smend (*Th.B* 27), Munich, 1965, pp. 13–64.
6. A brief biographical sketch of Wellhausen is given, with a critique of his general intellectual background and method, by F. Boschwitz, *Julius Wellhausen. Motive und Massstabe seiner Geschichtsschreibung*, Marburg, 1938, reprinted Darmstadt, 1968.
7. K. H. Graf, *Die geschichtlichen Bücher des Alten Testaments*, 1869, and in an essay entitled 'Die sogenannte Grundschrift des Pentateuchs', in *Archiv für Erforschung des Alten Testamentes*, 1869, pp. 466–477.
8. J. Wellhausen, *Prolegomena*, p. 3.
9. J. Wellhausen, *Skizzen und Vorarbeiten. II, Die Composition des Hexateuchs*, Berlin, 1885. Wellhausen's conclusions regarding the structure of the Hexateuch are also set out in his revisions to F. Bleek, *Einleitung in das Alte Testament*, fourth edition, Berlin, 1878, especially pp. 152–178.
10. Wellhausen's great interest in this subject is shown by his study *Die Pharisäer und die Saddacäer*, Greifswald, 1874; third edition, Göttingen, 1967.
11. J. Wellhausen, *Prolegomena*, p. 3.

12. A valuable study of the life and work of Hermann Gunkel is presented by W. Klatt, entitled, *Hermann Gunkel. Zu seiner Theologie der Religionsgeschichte und zur Entstehung der formgeschichtliche Methode, FRLANT* 100, Göttingen, 1969.

13. H. Gunkel, *Schöpfung und Chaos in Urzeit und Endzeit*, Göttingen, 1895.

14. Especially in an essay entitled 'Zur apokalyptischen Literatur', reprinted in *Skizzen und Vorarbeiten, VI*, 1899, pp. 215–249. The controversy is discussed by Klatt, *op. cit.*, pp. 70–74.

15. In 1903 Gunkel published a short study with the title, *Zum religionsgeschichtlicher Verständnis des Neuen Testaments, FRLANT* 1. Cf. also his essay entitled 'The "Historical Movement" in the Study of Religion', in *The Expository Times* 38, 1926–27, pp. 532–536.

16. H. Gunkel, *Genesis (HKAT* 1), Göttingen, 1901.

17. *The Legends of Genesis*, Chicago, 1901, reprinted with a new preface by W. F. Albright, New York, 1964.

18. The point is fully discussed by Klatt, *op. cit.*, pp. 106–116.

19. H. Gressmann, *Mose und seine Zeit, FRLANT* 18, Göttingen, 1913.

20. H. Gressmann, *Die älteste Geschichtschreibung und Prophetie Israels* (*SAT* II/1), Göttingen, 1910; second edition, 1921.

21. J. Wellhausen, *Prolegomena*, pp. 392–3.

22. H. Gressmann, *Mose und seine Zeit*, pp. 471 ff.

23. P. Volz, *Mose, Ein Beitrag zur Untersuchung über die Ursprünge der Israelitischen Religion*, Tübingen, 1907; second edition, *Mose und sein Werk*, 1932.

24. O. Procksch, *Das Nordhebräisch Sagenbuch. Die Elohimquelle*, Leipzig, 1906.

25. P. Volz and W. Rudolph, *Der Elohist als Erzähler. Ein Irrweg der Pentateuchkritik?*, *BZAW* 63, Berlin, 1933. Cf. also W. Rudolph, *Der 'Elohist' von Exodus bis Josua, BZAW* 68, Berlin 1938.

26. O. Eissfeldt, *Hexateuch-Synopse*, Leipzig, 1922; reprinted Darmstadt, 1962.

27. G. Fohrer, *An Introduction to the Old Testament*, London, 1970, pp. 159ff.

28. C. F. Burney, *The Book of Judges*, London, 1918, p. xlvi.

29. A. C. Welch, *The Code of Deuteronomy*, London, 1923.

30. A. Bentzen, *Die josianische Reform und ihre Voraussetzungen*, Copenhagen, 1926.

31. G. von Rad, *Das Gottesvolk im Deuteronomium, BWANT* III, 11, Stuttgart, 1929.

32. Y. Kaufmann, *The Religion of Israel from its Beginnings to the Babylonian Exile*, translated and abridged by M. Greenberg, London, 1961, pp. 175–200.

33. So M. Noth, *Leviticus*, English translation by J. E. Anderson, London, 1965. K. Elliger, *Leviticus, HAT* 4, Tübingen, 1966, pp. 9–20.

34. S. Mowinckel, *Le Décalogue*, Paris, 1927.

35. J. Pedersen, 'Passahfest und Passahlegende', in *ZAW* 52, 1934, pp. 161–. Cf. also *Israel*, III–IV, Copenhagen, 1940. Additional Note 1, 'The Crossing of the Reed Sea and the Paschal Legend', pp. 728–737.

36. G. Fohrer, *Überlieferung und Geschichte des Exodus*, in *BZAW* 91, Berlin, 1964.
37. A. Alt, *Die Ursprünge des Israelitischen Rechts*, Leipzig, 1934; English translation by R. A. Wilson 'The Origins of Israelite Law', in *Essays on Old Testament History and Religion*, Oxford, 1966, pp. 79–132.
38. G. E. Mendenhall, 'Ancient Oriental and Biblical Law', in *BA* 17, 1954, pp. 26–46.
39. G. von Rad, *Die Priesterschrift im Hexateuch, BWANT* IV, 13, Stuttgart, 1934.
40. G. von Rad, *Das formgeschichtliche Problem des Hexateuch, BWANT* IV, 24, Stuttgart, 1938. English translation by E. W. T. Dicken in *The Problem of the Hexateuch and Other Essays*, London, 1965, pp. 1–78.
41. So. L. Rost, 'Das kleine geschichtliche Credo', *Das kleine Credo und andere Studien zum Alten Testament*, Heidelberg, 1965, pp. 11–25. Th.C. Vriezen, 'The Credo in the Old Testament', in *Studies in the Psalms. Die ou Testamentiese Werkgemeenschap in Suid Afrika*, edited by A. H. van Zyl, Potchefstrom, 1963, pp. 5–17.
42. M. Noth, *Das Buch Josua, HAT 7*, Tübingen, 1938; second edition, 1953, pp. 7–17.
43. M. Noth, *Überlieferungsgeschichtliche Studien*, Halle, 1943; reprinted Tübingen, 1957.
44. M. Noth, *Überlieferungsgeschichte des Pentateuch*, Stuttgart, 1948. English translation by B. W. Anderson, *A History of Pentateuchal Traditions*, Englewood Cliffs, 1972.
45. I. Engnell, *Gamla Testamentet. En traditionshistorisk Inledning*, Stockholm, 1945. Cf. also his essay 'The Pentateuch', in *Critical Essays on the Old Testament*, translated by J. T. Willis, London, 1970, pp. 50–67.
46. The point is discussed, and examples given in favour of the view that P was a distinct author, by S. Mowinckel, *Erwägungen zur Pentateuchquellenfrage*, Oslo, 1964, pp. 16–20. The position advocated by Engnell had earlier been tentatively suggested by P. Volz in P. Volz and W. Rudolph, *Der Elohist als Erzähler*, pp. 135ff.

3

Interpreting the Historical Books

In the preface to his *Prolegomena* Wellhausen tells how in his student days he was attracted to the historical and prophetic books of the Old Testament, but felt troubled because of his unfamiliarity with the Law, which, he had been taught, was presupposed by them:

> At last I took courage and made my way through Exodus, Leviticus and Numbers, and even through Knobel's commentary to these books. But it was in vain that I looked for the light which was to be shed from this source on the historical and prophetical books. On the contrary, my enjoyment of the latter was marred by the Law; it did not bring them any nearer me, but intruded itself uneasily, like a ghost that makes a noise indeed, but is not visible and really effects nothing.[1]

Thus Wellhausen concluded that the historical books could not be properly interpreted in the light of the Law, rather they pointed to the relatively late development of it. This led him on to the recognition that the Hexateuch comprised four main sources, each of which belonged to a particular age of the religious development of Israel. In line with this Wellhausen came to recognize that each age, in writing the history of its own past, interpreted the traditions about this in its own way. Hence we could see in the Hexateuch how Israel had viewed its origins in one way in the ninth and eighth centuries, and in another in the fourth and fifth. Just as the sources of the Hexateuch reflect the various stages of development of the cultic and social institutions of Israel, so the historical books which follow this contain material from different ages of religious development, and reflect a comparable progress of religious ideas and outlook.

On the basis of such a recognition, and after surveying the historical development of Israel's religious institutions, Wellhausen turned to the books of 1 and 2 Chronicles where, as he put it, 'the matter is clearest'.[2] Although the Chronicler's work also included the books of Ezra and Nehemiah, much of it surveyed the same period that is also covered in the books of Samuel and Kings, which provided its major sources. Whereas, however, these latter books had been edited in the Babylonian exile, the Chronicler's history came from fully three hundred years later, after the fall of the Persian kingdom.

> See what Chronicles has made out of David! The founder of the kingdom has become the founder of the temple and the public worship, the king and hero at the head of his companions in arms has become the singer and master of ceremonies at the head of a swarm of priests and Levites; his clearly cut figure has become a feeble holy picture, seen through a cloud of incense![3]

> The alterations and additions of Chronicles are all traceable to the same fountainhead—the Judaising of the past, in which otherwise the people of that day would have been unable to recognize their ideal[4].

In this way Wellhausen was able to show that the work of the Chronicler was a historical document of a very distinctive kind, for it very openly and demonstrably viewed the past in terms of the aims and ideals of its own day. Yet when we turn to the other historical books of the Old Testament, those of Judges, 1 and 2 Samuel and 1 and 2 Kings, we find that the same judgement holds essentially true, although it is not the ideals of the Chronicler's age which this time obtrude so markedly.

So far as the book of Joshua was concerned, we have seen that Wellhausen accepted that this was composed of a continuation of the source documents traceable in the preceding books of the Pentateuch. However when we turn to the book of Judges we discover that this contains very early historical narratives, but that these have been subjected to a comprehensive revision:

> In short what is usually given out as the peculiar theocratic element in the history of Israel is the element which has been introduced by the redaction.[5]

As to the character of this 'revision', or 'redaction', Wellhausen was in no doubt. It was 'Deuteronomistic', since its essential assumption was that the Deuteronomic law stood behind the events narrated, and provided a standard by which they could be judged. In proceeding to the books of Samuel, Wellhausen noted the presence of the same 'last revision', although not in so marked a fashion, except where it came to deal with the question of the introduction of the monarchy in I Samuel 7–12, where the Deuteronomistic ideals of a theocracy are very prominently set out. In the books of Kings however: 'the last revision works most unrestrictedly'.[6]

In this way Wellhausen was able to show, not only in the case of the Chronicler but also in Judges, Samuel and Kings, that the views and distinctive religious ideals of a particular age have been impressed on the earlier sources. In the case of the Chronicler's history these were the ideals of the Persian period, but in Judges, 1 and 2 Samuel and 1 and 2 Kings the ideals were those that had arisen in the Babylonian exile which bore strong affinity with the ideas and aims to be found in the book of Deuteronomy. There were, of course, some points of difference, and Wellhausen could claim:

> If, accordingly, we are fully justified in calling the revision Deuteronomistic, this means no more than that it came into existence under the influence of Deuteronomy which pervaded the whole century of the exile. The difference between Deuteronomistic and Deuteronomic is one not of time only but of matter as well.[7]

In this way Wellhausen provided an important means of assessing the historical worth and reliability of the historical books by identifying the character of the redaction which had been imposed upon earlier source material. He thereby left the latter more clearly isolated and free to provide its own witness. As to the worth of this historical source material itself Wellhausen recognized its varying quality. In some cases, as in the Court History of David which Wellhausen identified in 2 Samuel 9–20, he found a major source of immense value to the historian, whilst in other examples, as in the cases of the prophetic narratives concerning Elijah, the tradition had greatly exaggerated the influence of the prophet.

In accord with his overall aim of attaining a picture of the actual progress of Israel's history and religious development, Wellhausen's attention was concentrated upon the problem of getting at the contents of the earliest narrative materials by setting the redactional element aside. This concern to dig through to the earliest reliable historical evidence continued to command the major interest of most other scholars who followed in the wake of Wellhausen. After the contribution of the 'last revision' had been set aside it was clear that a considerable variety of documents had been used, and this was further borne out by the fact that the books of Kings refer explicitly to a number of sources which were evidently available in documentary form. So also in Judges and 1 and 2 Samuel it is evident that written sources from more than one age have been employed. In view of the success achieved by the documentary hypothesis in unravelling the problems of the Hexateuch, it is not surprising that a similar approach should have been expected to offer a prospect of a comparable achievement in solving the problems of the books from Judges to 2 Kings. In the case of the Chronicler the situation was different since it was certain that the major source for 1 and 2 Chronicles had been provided by the earlier accounts contained in the books of Samuel and Kings.

Such an underlying conviction led the German scholar Karl Budde (1850–1935) to try to carry over into the study of the sources of Judges and 1 and 2 Samuel the same general approach that had been so widely acclaimed in regard to the Hexateuch. Born in Bensburg, near Cologne, Budde taught in the universities of Bonn, Strasbourg and Marburg. His work achieved wide popularity in Britain and America, especially through his volume on the *History of Israel's Religion to the Exile*.[8] He has probably been best remembered for his advocacy of the 'Kenite hypothesis', which argued that Mosaic Yahwism had been adopted into Israel from the Kenites, to which tribe Moses was related by marriage.[9] For the progress of the interpretation of the Old Testament, and especially in regard to questions of methodology, a significant feature of his research is to be found in his examination of the sources of the books of Judges and 1 and 2 Samuel[10] which was further developed in his commentaries on these books. He argued that much of the source material has been drawn from the same J and E sources as are to be found in the Hexateuch. As a result we should recognize that these major sources carried their history of Israel's fortunes right on up to the time when they themselves had been composed. This was not to deny that other written sources had also been used, but it established a claim that the provenance and character of much of the material could be understood from what had already been established in regard to the Hexateuch. Going beyond what Wellhausen had argued, Budde now claimed that the new literary criticism could solve the problem of the sources of the remaining books of the Former Prophets (Judges to 2 Kings). Such a view was taken up by other scholars, notably O. Eissfeldt in a study of the sources of the books of Judges[12] and 1 and 2 Samuel[13] and from this has obtained a wide currency in the study of the Old Testament.

Not all scholars have been convinced that we can trace the presence of the J and E sources in these historical books, but nonetheless it was natural to look for extended documentary sources of a kind similar to, if not identical with, those of the Hexateuch. This was the view set out by the Scottish scholar A. R. S. Kennedy whose commentary on the books of

1 and 2 Samuel in the *Century Bible* was among the most successful of the volumes in that series.[14] Kennedy sought to trace several extended written sources which could be conveniently labelled by various letters of the alphabet.

In spite of many such attempts to understand the structure of the historical books by resorting to a theory of their compilation out of several documents of this kind, it has proved difficult to reach a conclusion that has been as generally convincing to scholarship as was the case with the Hexateuch. It is only an assumption that the J and E documents can be traced in these other books, since it has not been possible to establish positive arguments in favour of such an identification. Furthermore there are lacking signs of clear continuity between the sources of the different books, and attention can more readily be drawn to the separate narratives and the way they have been collected around certain great figures, notably Samuel, Saul and David. In 1910 H. Gressmann published a short commentary on the books of Samuel and Kings in the series *Die Schriften des Alten Testaments*.[15] He argued that we must interpret the individual narratives by themselves, as Gunkel's *gattungsgeschichtliche* method had established for Genesis. This still left room for the conclusion that these narratives had subsequently undergone a Deuteronomistic redaction, as Wellhausen had argued, although Gressmann was not much interested in this. The commentary showed that no really helpful information about a particular narrative in these books can be gleaned by endeavouring to identify it as stemming from J or E, or some document closely related to them.

Gressmann's study thereby put a new light on the problem of the sources of the books from Judges to 2 Kings. It was eventually to lead to a change of outlook which gravely weakened the hypothesis that the Hexateuchal sources were to be found in them. Before this happened, however, a much fuller investigation had to take place into the way in which the short narrative units which Gressmann had concentrated on, had been combined to form larger complexes. Meanwhile other aspects of the interpretation of the historical books were commanding interest and attention.

In one period of Israel's history in particular the evidence of the Old Testament was notably limited, so that additional evidence from external sources was eminently desirable. This was the age of Israel's conquest of Canaan, which is described primarily in the book of Joshua, but for which the book of Judges also offers important evidence. In Joshua the sum of the various narratives only account for the acquisition of a relatively small central part of the land that at one time belonged to Israel. The books of Judges and 1 Samuel, however, show that for some considerable time after its occupation of the land, Israel was forced to share it with others, including Philistines and Canaanites as well as smaller ethnic groups. Not until the time of David was anything like a full control of the territory obtained. The eminent desirability of relating Israel's entry into Canaan with what was otherwise known of Near Eastern history from Egypt and Mesopotamia, naturally encouraged scholars to investigate this period more fully. Separate treatments of the problem were offered by C. F. Burney[16] and J. Garstang.[17] Much later, and in the light of more extensive archaeological evidence, H. H. Rowley[18] sought to shed light on the problem. At first it did not appear too much to hope that it would be possible to offer a precise date for the Israelite overthrow of Canaanite Jericho which could be linked more generally with the date of the Israelite conquest. Yet the inconclusiveness of the Old Testament source material, and the severe limitations of the available techniques of archaeological interpretation, resulted in little convincing clarification.

Bearing this particular problem in mind, we can turn our attention to the work of a scholar who was to provide a remarkably brilliant series of essays upon the problems of Israelite history, and who was able to introduce some important new methodological considerations into its investigation. This was Albrecht Alt (1883–1956), a native of Stübach and, like several other scholars, the son of a pastor. Born in 1883, Alt was first elected to a professorship at Basel in 1913. Before then, however, two events had taken place which were to have a profound effect upon his career. The first was the Bible-Babel controversy of 1901 and the years which followed, which we have already had occasion to notice. The second was the founding in 1904 of the German Evangelical Institute for the Study of the Holy Land in Palestine.

With regard to the Bible-Babel controversy, Alt reasoned that one aspect of the error of attempting to press so heavily the Babylonian background of the Old Testament was the false assumption that outside influence upon Israel's life and religion had been exerted almost exclusively from Mesopotamia. The Old Testament itself bore ample testimony to the fact that very real and early contacts had existed between Israel and her southern neighbour Egypt. It is worthy of note therefore that Alt's *Habilitationsschrift* was devoted to the subject of *Israel und Ägypten*.[19] In this he investigated the wide range of historical relationships which had existed between Israel and Egypt throughout the Old Testament period.

The founding of the German Institute in Jerusalem enabled Alt to spend time studying there in the years immediately before the First World War. It led him to develop an interest in the special problems of the topography and historical geography of Palestine. This had a quite immediate consequence in that during the war he served there in the German oriental army, first as a medical officer and later as a cartographer. From the close personal knowledge of the land which he obtained, Alt was able to approach the problems of Israel's history from a new direction. This resulted in his establishing what has been termed a 'historico-geographical' method. Basic features of topography and climate establish a given range of possibilities for the economy and communications of a region which do not radically alter unless there are major changes in the culture or the population. Even within a changing pattern of political relationships many features remain constant. Not only so, but a given picture, or map, of the political and social development of a region acquires a distinctive historical stamp which marks it as belonging to a particular age. This fact can be readily seen in any Bible atlas which shows the political situation in Palestine at different biblical periods. As a result a knowledge of the geography of a territory is able to provide important clues regarding its history. When coupled with a knowledge of the political geography existing at various times the whole method can provide invaluable evidence regarding the background of events.

One of Alt's earliest essays, published in the *Festschrift* for R. Kittel in 1913, was devoted to the list of regional boundaries contained in 1 Kings 4, which describes the administrative districts established by Solomon.[20] In it he raised a number of considerations concerning the structure and geographical limits of the Israelite state which were later to concern him again on several occasions. Prominent among these was the place and function of kingship in Israel and Judah. Alt argued that the monarchy arose in Israel as a dual institution, binding together in the person of the one Davidic king the two kingdoms of Israel and Judah. These had originally existed as separate tribal associations, and reverted to this separateness under Rehoboam. Evidence for this was found by Alt in the successive stages by which David had risen to the throne, first of Judah, and then subsequently of Israel. In later essays Alt developed this further to trace in the two sister kingdoms two different conceptions of kingship, one dynastic and tied to the family of David, and the other charismatic and tied to no one family or dynasty.

These early studies by Alt were the first of an immense number of similar articles and studies, which are of great importance for the interpretation of Israel's history and historical literature. It is of particular interest to see therefore how, at the outset of his career, Alt showed certain interests, and established particular methods, which were to reappear later with increasing clarity and conviction. On two particular issues the further development of Alt's researches was to lead to solutions being proposed for problems which are of great significance and complexity. The first is that which we have already mentioned concerning the Israelite conquest of Canaan, whilst the second deals with the organization of Israel in Palestine before the monarchy.

We have already noted the great difficulty that historians were encountering in seeking to clarify the events surrounding the Israelite conquest of Canaan as it is described in the book of Joshua. The much celebrated archaeological excavations at Jericho had provided no adequate basis for attaining a convincing reconstruction of what had taken place and when. As a result, scholars were becoming increasingly attracted to the view that there had been not one, but two conquests of Canaan, one from the south and one from the east led by Joshua. In an essay published in 1925[21] Alt set the whole problem in a fresh, and very different perspective. He began his examination with a study of the evidence from external sources of the situation which had existed in Palestine in the latter half of the second millennium BC. The decisive importance of his attention to Egyptian sources and their relevance for the study of the Old Testament immediately revealed itself.

Although the evidence was scattered, and provided only a partial picture of the Palestinian situation, Alt was able to reconstruct an account of the formation of the kingdom of Israel. It showed small Canaanite city-states, under Egyptian hegemony, with other population elements spread throughout the rural areas and only partially controlled by the rulers of the cities. These were of mixed character, and made up largely of sheep-farming, tent-dwelling, beduin, who moved their pastures with the changing seasons. The evidence showed a steady and prolonged migration of such people from further east into the settled Palestinian land. Alt's thesis was essentially that it was this prolonged settlement of such sheep-farming beduin in Canaan which came retrospectively to be viewed as a conquest of the land. The event of the occupation of the land was not a concentrated and planned invasion, which could be ascribed to one particular date, but the piecemeal taking over of thinly inhabited territory. The fighting associated with it was the random skirmishing which resulted from local disagreements about land, and from the varying degrees of pressure exerted by the Canaanite city states. It is these local skirmishes which have been recorded in the books of Joshua and Judges and which have been viewed by a later age as the concerted action of all Israel.

In conjunction with this new approach towards finding a solution of the problem of Israel's settlement in Palestine, Alt considered the complex historical problem concerning Israel's emergence as a territorial state under a monarchy. In many respects the problems concerning the settlement in the land and the formation of the Israelite state were related, since both aspects of the national history hinged upon the question of the nature of the people's social and political organization before the acquisition of full national status. Here Alt pointed to the importance of Israel's tribal structure and the deep mark this had left upon the people and their history. Once again the distinctive historico-geographical method which he had initiated contributed an important insight. In the Festschrift for E. Sellin of 1927 he published an essay on the list of tribal boundaries contained in the book of Joshua,[22] which is comparable in its interest and scope to that presented in 1913 for R. Kittel on the districts of Solomon's kingdom. In it he argued that the boundary list was not, as had hitherto been supposed, a late idealized composition from the post-exilic Priestly writer, but an early official composition which conformed essentially to the situation of the tribal settlements before the monarchy had been introduced into Israel.

Alt was to return to the question of this list again and to develop and modify this suggestion, but in 1927 it provided a new basis for consideration of the question of Israel's pre-monarchic structure and organization. One feature which particularly stood out was the fact that the unity of Israel was not established by any developed form of inter-tribal political organization, nor yet by geographical features, for some of the tribes had been seriously cut off from the others. It was the common worship of Yahweh which bound the tribes to each other and encouraged them to a sense of mutual loyalty. In a short article on Israel published in the second edition of the dictionary, *Die Religion in Geschichte und Gegenwart*,[23] Alt drew attention to a comparable picture of such a religious bond to the early Greek and Italian communities which had existed as amphictyonies.

The fuller elaboration of this hypothesis was subsequently explored and brilliantly worked out by Alt's pupil M. Noth, but it is important to recognize its roots in the whole context of Alt's understanding of the nature of Israel's settlement in Palestine. In a number of significant respects Alt's views regarding the two types of monarchy which were to be found respectively in Israel and Judah, and the claim that Israel had at one time been organized as an amphictyony, have their origins in his historico-geographical method. This lies at the heart of a new era of Old Testament study made possible by the geographical and archaeological study of the land of Palestine. Although Alt himself never wrote a complete history of Israel, he established a basis for doing so which reached far beyond the confines of the methods established by Wellhausen.

The historical researches of Alt were not primarily concerned with the literary problems of the historical books, although they affected these at a number of points. Alt regarded the lists of boundaries, which are to be found at several points, as authentic documents from particular periods of Israel's history, albeit not necessarily the periods to which the history now ascribed them. They were not, however, late idealized compositions drawn up by an age which looked back upon a distant past from which no authentic records had been kept.

The most significant further development of the literary study of the books of 1 and 2 Samuel took place through the further exploration of the method of *Gattungsgeschichte*. Already in his study of the sources of the historical books Wellhausen had pointed to the connected character of the stories of intrigue and rebellion in David's court. This 'Court History' covered 2 Samuel 9–20. In 1926 L. Rost published a detailed study of the literary structure and purpose of this narrative,[24] which he now argued was to be understood as a Succession Narrative, since it had continued originally to tell of Solomon's accession to the throne of David. This continuation was to be found in 1 Kings 1–2, which carried the story of David's court troubles a stage further to show their outcome. Although scholars such as Wellhausen and Budde had also pointed to the connected nature of this material, what was significant in Rost's treatment was the argument that the study of the separate narrative incidents needed to be supplemented by a recognition of the overall redactional purpose which they had been made to serve. What Rost was in fact doing was to develop Gressmann's approach, recognizing that the separate narratives have been strung together into chains, or complexes. Rost noted that a similar complex of separate narrative incidents had been formed into the story of the history and journeys of the Ark.[25] The importance of these blocks of narrative was recognized by A. Alt, in a study of the origin of the Israelite state, and has been further taken up and examined in more recent years. Rost's study marks the beginning of a growing awareness that the books of 1 and 2 Samuel contain extended collections of stories about particular figures, which were formed into a connected history at a comparatively early period. As a result the notion that we were faced here with an interweaving of documentary sources on the pattern of the Pentateuch became obsolete. The problem of sources had to be seen in a different light in these books.

In this connection we should note also a contribution from a Scandinavian scholar along very similar lines. This was I. Hylander, who published in 1932 a study of the complex of stories involving the figures of Samuel and Saul.[26] This carried still further the examination of the individual units, and sought to trace the history through which they had passed before being combined into an overall history, and finally woven into their present position in the book of 1 Samuel.

In doing so he noted the tendencies of the various traditions regarding these figures, and the ways in which these tendencies were reflected in the processes of redaction. As an essay in criticism it grew directly out of the insights and methods initiated by Gunkel, and established a technique of what would now be called redaction criticism. The appearance of redaction criticism marked a further step in the abandonment of the attempt to solve the problems posed by these books upon the lines of extended documentary sources.

A further consequence of the studies by Rost and Hylander was to make it increasingly clear that the historical books were religious writings, and that in their origin and redaction they were intended to serve religious ends. The idea that the events which they reported could readily be reconstructed by considering the questions of the age and reliability of the underlying sources was increasingly shown to be too simple a view.[27] It was necessary rather to investigate the particular setting and tendencies displayed by the narrative accounts before their real worth could be understood. Perhaps too, when viewed in retrospect, we can see that the assumptions and insights of traditio-historical study of the Old Testament historical literature brought out the religious, rather than the purely historical, side of its contents.

This in itself posed something of a challenge to the marked emphasis upon the specifically historical aspects of the study of the Old Testament which had assumed paramount importance in many theological curricula. Studies of the history of Israel and of its religion had in many cases replaced the more overtly theological aspects of the Old Testament, yet scholarship itself was being made to realize that what the Old

Testament presented as history was given from a markedly theological standpoint. The literature had been written as a witness to the religious and political life of Israel, and at all levels, from the short narrative units through to the more extended literary complexes and their redaction, this distinctive religious tendency was evident. At first it had appeared important to recognize this religious interest, or bias, simply in order to set it aside in reaching back to the underlying events of Israel's history. Yet this approach was increasingly being shown to be inadequate, and a new awareness was emerging that it was necessary to examine the religious and theological side of the historical books in order to appreciate their true character. Within the study of Old Testament theology this was eventually to lead to a very distinctive understanding of biblical history as salvation history (*Heilsgeschichte*).

The scholar who took up and developed most extensively the methods and fundamental insights established by Alt was M. Noth. Born in Dresden in 1902, Noth became professor in Königsberg in 1930, after having taught in Greifswald and Leipzig. In 1928 he published an examination of the form, structure and significance of Israelite personal names[28] which provided a significant source of understanding for his next work. This was a detailed presentation of the hypothesis that early Israel's organization was closely similar to that of the early Greek and Italian amphictyonies. Entitled *Das System der Zwölf Stämme Israels* (*The System of the Twelve Tribes of Israel*)[29] this study of the tribal organization of ancient Israel built up Alt's suggestion regarding its nature and elaborated this with great detail and care.

The earlier study of Israelite names provided important material by showing that several of the tribal names could only have arisen on the soil of Canaan, and thus Israel as a twelve tribe amphictyony must have come into existence after it had settled in Palestine. Such an amphictyony was essentially a union of independent communities bound through their common worship of a god at a central shrine, and Noth argued that in ancient Israel this shrine had been that of the ark. The geographical importance of the city of Shechem in the life of early Israel was accounted for on the assumption that the ark had at one time been kept there. The fixity of the number of tribes at twelve was seen by Noth to derive from the need for each tribe to supply the priestly service for the central sanctuary for one month in each year. Once again developing the views of Alt, Noth saw a close relationship between Israel's organization as an amphictyony and its distinctive traditions of law, since a basis of common legal obligations was the major consequence of the mutual obligation to worship the same God. The central officer of the tribal union was the law-speaker who was responsible for ensuring that the legal and ethical demands of the worship of this God were accepted by all the member tribes. At a later stage Noth developed this idea still further in seeking to trace the special provenance of the Book of the Covenant of Exodus 20:22–23:19.

Building upon this foundation hypothesis of Noth's regarding Israel's organization as an amphictyony a considerable range of further studies concerning the history of Israel's worship, laws and prophecy has been developed. So much has this been the case that a very wide area of the Old Testament literature has, in one way or another, come to be associated with such a hypothesis. Undoubtedly such an accumulation of hypotheses based upon a foundation which itself only remains a hypothesis has gone too far to remain convincing. It has resulted in making the notion of an Israelite amphictyony a kind of blanket hypothesis by which too many other features of Israelite life, sometimes standing at variance with one another, have been interpreted. The final product has been to spread confusion rather than light. Such excesses, however, go far beyond the more modest confines of the hypothesis as Noth presented it. Whilst with the progress of scholarship a number of important criticisms have arisen to challenge such a view, it has proved very difficult to offer a convincing alternative understanding of early Israelite political and religious organization. One very important consequence of the subject been to draw considerable attention to the fact that Israel retained a strong and vitalizing memory of its existence as God's people before it had existed as a state with a land of its own. In the course of its history this memory was to have very important and far-reaching consequences, and has continued to do so down to the present day. Israel's election as God's people has not been tied to its existence in any one political, territorial or religious form.

It is not surprising that Noth's interest in the structure of early Israel, and his concern to build upon the foundations laid by Alt, should have led to his being invited to write a commentary on the book of Joshua. Noth's volume first appeared in 1938.[30] In it he greatly developed and enlarged upon some of the conclusions reached by Alt in a number of essays regarding the lists of tribal boundaries and cities contained in Joshua 13–19 and the distinctive character of the stories of Joshua 3–9. These latter were of importance since they provided a key factor in the understanding of the Israelite occupation of Canaan as a conquest.

However it was clear to Alt and Noth that these stories had at one

43

time had a more local reference and were aetiological in their character. This meant that they had arisen in order to explain certain basic features of topography and local cultic practice. Noth could not find in them any evidence of their having once formed part of either the J or E sources. Developing Alt's fresh understanding of the nature of the material contained in Joshua 13–19, Noth now argued that the major Pentateuchal sources of J, E and P were not clearly evident in Joshua at all. This meant that the long-held view that these were essentially 'Hexateuchal' sources was not true in the sense in which it had usually been claimed.

The fuller consequences of this fresh study of Joshua were subsequently related by Noth to the wider problem of the sources and editorial structure of the books of Judges, 1 and 2 Samuel and 1 and 2 Kings. This was closely connected with Noth's reconsideration of the observation which Wellhausen had made regarding the Deuteronomistic character of their 'last revision'. When worked out in connection with the new understanding of the longer complexes of historical material in the books of Samuel, Noth was able in 1943 to set out a very attractive alternative picture of the origin and structure of the entire historical narrative from Joshua to 2 Kings.[31] In this he argued that these books were not separate compositions, but rather formed one continuous Deuteronomistic History which began with the law book of Deuteronomy and extended to the end of 2 Kings. This is why in the work the law of Deuteronomy is regarded as expressing the divine will by which the subsequent account of the rise and fall of Israel is judged and interpreted. Deuteronomy 1–3 had been composed as the historical preface to this major piece of history-writing. Subsequently some additions had been made, notably in Judges 1, Joshua 13–19 and Joshua 24.

In general, Noth's fresh understanding of the Former Prophets, as these historical books were known in the Hebrew canon, marked a notable advance over Wellhausen's view to which in many respects it was quite directly related. In a large number of features it appears to be superior and more convincing than the earlier, only partially successful, attempts to find in these books traces of the Pentateuchal sources. It has stood out very distinctively as a major contribution to the evaluation of the historical books of the Old Testament. It provided Noth himself with a significantly new understanding of these books as a step towards his ultimate goal of writing the history of the people of Israel in the biblical period. This was a task in which Noth summed up a wide range of results from his own researches and those of his teacher Alt.[32] Noth's original essay on the Deuteronomistic History combined with it a fresh evaluation of the work of the Chronicler in regard to its sources, method and purpose. That this had formed a continuous work comprising 1 and 2 Chronicles, Ezra and Nehemiah, had long been recognized, so that here Noth's contribution was less original in its conclusions. Overall Noth's researches into the composition of the major historical writings of the Old Testament outside the Pentateuch pointed to two great works; that of the Deuteronomist and that of the Chronicler.

As a historian, Noth's work falls into a pattern of scholarship which is closely related to, and dependent on, the methods and insights of Alt, although this is in no way to belittle the great originality of the results Noth achieved. Where Alt's work had been scattered and disseminated in a host of articles and short monographs published in many volumes of learned journals and academic series, Noth incorporated his conclusions into a *History of Israel* which has become one of the most widely used theological text-books in Europe. The wide use of relevant geographical and archaeological data, coupled with information drawn from rediscovered annals and chronicles of the ancient world, brought to light a picture of Israel's history which was different in a great many ways from that presented earlier by Wellhausen. Whereas Wellhausen had concentrated almost exclusively upon the Old Testament source material, and had aimed chiefly at offering a convincing and credible picture of the history of Israel's religious institutions, Noth strove for something that approaches very much more closely to a 'secular' history of the people. Hence he considered much more extensively the problems of Israel's political structure and development. This deepening awareness of the wide range of problems involved in the task of writing a history of Israel is an eloquent expression of the way in which the nature of the task had been set out with greater precision with the progress of scholarship.

Noth's work on Israel's history brought to a culmination the insights and endeavours which had begun half a century before with the introduction of Alt's 'historico-geographical' method. That it was only a step on the way towards a yet fuller knowledge of its subject is obvious from the very nature and complexities of Old Testament scholarship.

After a period of wide acceptance among scholars, Noth's view that early Israel's structure and organization could best be understood after the analogy of the Greek amphictyonies has run into increasing criticism.[33] Insufficient Old Testament evidence to show that the ark represented Israel's central shrine and was at one time kept at Shechem has been raised as an objection to such a hypothesis. Similarly the very limited evidence to support the claim that on occasions the amphictyony acted in unison for purposes of military defence poses further problems for it. It has led R. Smend[34] to argue that the institution of the holy war was originally separate from the tribal federation, which represents a later, and only very imperfectly developed, organization. Uncertainties too regarding the existence of official tribal representatives at amphictyonic councils and of the role played by the amphictyony in the development of a truly Israelite tradition of law have all contributed further towards stimulating a re-appraisal of this important hypothesis. The major difficulty, however, has been that of finding a better explanation for the undoubted religious bond that held the Israelite tribes together before the rise of a territorial state under David and Solomon. Other problems posed by Noth's understanding of the early growth of the Pentateuchal tradition have added more stimulus to the search for a different approach to the task of writing Israel's history. Especially scholars have sought one which leans less heavily upon the view that early Israel was an amphictyony established in Canaan.

In this respect mention may be made of the important effort of S. Herrmann, another of Alt's pupils, to carry through the task of writing Israel's history in the Old Testament period, without assuming the various features which have become linked with the amphictyony hypothesis.[35]

From another side altogether, however, the study of the historical writings of the Old Testament has begun to acquire a very different complexion. Since the work of J. Wellhausen it has been almost taken for granted that the appropriate way of interpreting these books is to recover as accurately as possible a knowledge of the events which they report. This is why there has been a pre-eminent concern with sources, with historical methodology generally, and with the contribution of the historical books towards the writing of Israel's history. Yet the books from Joshua to 2 Kings are classed in the Hebrew canon as the Former Prophets, and the very presence in the Old Testament of the Chronicler's work, with its much revised presentation of the age of the monarchy, shows that the interests of those who preserved and canonized the Old Testament writings lay elsewhere than in a strictly formal history. This fact was of course recognized from the very beginnings of a critical approach to the Old Testament.

However such studies as that by L. Rost on the Succession Narrative have highlighted the way in which important parts of the Old Testament historical literature had been composed to support and interpret various basic institutions of Israel, in this case the Davidic monarchy with its principle of dynastic succession. G. von Rad devoted an essay to this historical narrative in which he was concerned not particularly with the factual events which lay behind it, but with its whole theology of history and its conception of the divine activity in the world.[36] Much later R. N. Whybray also considered the same narrative from the point of view of its relationship to the ideas and ideals of early Israelite wisdom.[37] We may note also that from the very different interests and standpoint of structural anthropology E. R. Leach has examined the form of the account of Solomon's succession with almost complete disregard for the questions of historicity which it raises.[38] All in all such studies are significant because they are symptomatic of a growing awareness that such historical narratives cannot be said to be adequately interpreted simply in terms of their historicity and general factual reliability. They are religious documents which were primarily intended to serve a religious purpose.

A similar recognition applies more broadly to the Deuteronomistic History as a whole, and also to that of the Chronicler, as even Wellhausen had so pointedly affirmed. These documents were written at particular points in Israel's religious development when some historical re-appraisal of the past was felt to be needful. Whilst Noth devoted a relatively small proportion of his study of these narratives to the questions of their underlying theological purpose, other scholars have viewed them much more directly from this point of view. Why were they written, and what particular ends were they meant to serve? In this regard we may note how central a part is played in von Rad's understanding of Old Testament theology by the claim that it is expressed in the form of a theological interpretation of history. The works of the Deuteronomist and the Chronicler, therefore, present us with very profound interpretations of Israel's understanding of its divine election. They reflect Israel's sense of standing before God, and express in their own ways Israel's hope for its future as a people. Other scholars have also turned their attention to considering the historical books of the Old Testament from this perspective, recognizing that an investigation of their sources and historical reliability are not the only questions about them which we need to ask.

In this regard we may consider the significance of the narrative of David's rise, in view of the great importance attached to its witness by

A. Alt as a major source for our knowledge of the rise of the Israelite state. He regarded it as of inestimable value for a recovery of the distinctive character of the institution of monarchy into Israel.[39] He dated the document no later than the age of Solomon. More recently several studies have been devoted to it, of which the fullest and most imposing has been that by the Danish scholar J. H. Grønbaek.[40] Grønbaek claims for it a rather greater compass than Rost had done, finding its beginning in 1 Samuel: 15. Even more significant in its consequences, is the fact that Grønbaek dates it after the disruption of the united monarchy at Solomon's death. The latter point is of considerable importance for the light it sheds upon the particular religious and political interests of the author. At a host of places Grønbaek notes its concern to justify the actions of David in the eyes of the Benjaminites, in view of the unexpected political situation which had arisen when the old tribal territories of Judah and Benjamin were forged into the new kingdom of Judah.

It is of interest to reflect that Wellhausen began his critical study of the Old Testament with the historical books. By seeking to find what light they could bring to bear upon the history of the Law, or the Law upon them, he became aware of their immense importance for our knowledge of the rise and development of Israel. The fact that they provide something of a test by which the other literature, especially that of the Pentateuch, can be judged as to its date and presuppositions, remains of great importance. It is clear that these books provide us with an indispensable basis of knowledge for understanding the history of Israel and its religion. Yet such a recognition can easily lead us to forget that these books were not written simply to record the past, but in order to shed light and meaning on their authors' present and to guide the way to a future which was still to come. It is only when we bear these considerations in mind that we are likely to appreciate sufficiently sympathetically the way in which these narratives interpret the past with such apparent freedom. At times they omit, revise, supplement, and even replace earlier material in the light of the subsequent movement of events. Their historical aims were clearly not those of a modern critical historian. Their aim was not to write an exact critical history, but to point to the action of God towards and within Israel, and to show how this had meaning for the present and future. In this way the historians of Israel have a relationship to the prophets which cannot be ignored. The fuller recognition of this relationship is one further aspect of the results of modern critical scholarship which has served to enrich our understanding of the historical books of the Old Testament.

1. J. Wellhausen, *Prolegomena*, p. 3.
2. J. Wellhausen, *Prolegomena*, p. 171.
3. J. Wellhausen, *Prolegomena*, p. 182.
4. J. Wellhausen, *Prolegomena*, p. 233.
5. J. Wellhausen, *Prolegomena*, p. 235.
6. J. Wellhausen, *Prolegomena*, p. 272.
7. J. Wellhausen, *Prolegomena*, p. 280.
8. K. Budde, 'Religion of Israel to the Exile' in *American Lectures on the History of Religions*, IV Series 1898–99, New York, 1899.
9. K. Budde, *ibid.*, pp. 1–38, 'Origin of the Yahweh-Religion'.
10. K. Budde, *Die Bücher Richter und Samuel, ihre Quellen und ihr Aufbau*, Giessen, 1890.
11. K. Budde, *Das Buch der Richter erklärt, KHAT* VII, Freiburg, Leipzig, Tübingen 1897. *Die Bucher Samuel erklärt KHAT* VIII, Tübingen and Leipzig, 1902.
12. O. Eissfeldt, *Die Quellen des Richterbuches*, Leipzig, 1925.
13. O. Eissfeldt, *Die Komposition der Samuelisbücher*, Leipzig, 1931.
14. A. R. S. Kennedy, '1 and 2 Samuel' *Century Bible* London, 1904.
15. H. Gressmann, *Die älteste Geschichtsschreibung und Prophetie Israels*, *SAT* I, 2, Göttingen, 1910, second edition, 1925.
16. C. F. Burney, *Israel's Settlement in Canaan. The Biblical Tradition and its Historical Background* (Schweich Lectures 1917), London, 1918.
17. J. Garstang, *Foundations of Bible History. Joshua and Judges*, London, 1931.
18. H. H. Rowley, *From Joseph to Joshua. Biblical Traditions in the Light of Archaeology* (Schweich Lectures 1948), London, 1950.
19. A. Alt, *Israel und Ägypten. Die politischen Beziehungen der Könige von Israel und Juda zu den Pharaonen. Nach den Quellen dargestellt*, *BWANT* 6, Leipzig, 1909.
20. A. Alt, 'Israels Gaue unter Salomo', in *Alttestamentliche Studien R. Kittel zum 60. Geburtstag dargebracht, BWANT* 13, Leipzig, pp. 1–19.
21. A. Alt, *Die Landnahme der Israeliten in Palaestina. Territorialgeschichtliche Studien*, Leipzig, 1925. (=*Kleine Schriften*, I, 1953, pp. 89–125). English translation by R. A. Wilson in *Essays on Old Testament History and Religion*, Oxford, 1966, pp. 133–169.
22. A. Alt, 'Das System der Stammesgrenzen im Buche Josua', in *Festschrift Ernst Sellin zum 60. Geburtstag dargebracht*, Leipzig, 1927, pp. 13–24. (= *Kleine Schriften*, I, pp. 193–202).
23. A. Alt, *Israel, politische Geschichte*, second edition, Vol. III, Tübingen, 1929, columns 437–442.
24. L. Rost, *Die Überlieferung von der Thronnachfolge Davids*, in *BWANT* III, 6 (=*Das kleine Credo und andere Studien zum Alten Testament*, Heidelberg, 1965, pp. 119–253).
25. L. Rost, *ibid.*, pp. 5–46 (*Das kleine Credo*, 122–159).
26. I. Hylander, *Der literarische Samuel-Saul-Komplex (I Samuel: 1–15). Traditionsgeschichtlich untersucht*, Uppsala, 1932.
27. There is a very pertinent comment to this effect by H. Gunkel in regard to the assumptions which underlay the Wellhausian approach: 'The school of

Wellhausen was and still is inclined, in its constructive historical work, to be too subservient to the literary documents, overlooking the fact that special precautions must be taken if the actual history is to be successfully reconstructed from the sources, however carefully these may have been sifted.' ('The Historical Movement' in *Study of Religion*, p. 533).

28. M. Noth, *Die Israelitischen Personennamen im Rahmen der gemeinsemitischen Namengebung*, in *BWANT* III, 10, Stuttgart, 1928; reprint Hildesheim, 1966.

29. M. Noth, *Das System der Zwölf Stämme Israels* in *BWANT* IV, 1, Stuttgart, 1930.

30. M. Noth, *Das Buch Josua* (*HAT* 7), Tübingen, 1938; second edition 1953.

31. M. Noth, *Überlieferungsgeschichtliche Studien*, Halle, 1943; reprinted Tübingen, 1957.

32. M. Noth, *Geschichte Israels*, first edition, Göttingen, 1950. English translation revised by P. R. Ackroyd, *The History of Israel*, second edition, London, 1960.

33. A criticism of this hypothesis is made by A. D. H. Mayes, *Israel in the Period of the Judges* (*SBT* Second Series 29), London, 1974, where reference to other studies along this line is made.

34. R. Smend, *Jahwekrieg und Stämmebund* (*FRLANT* 84), Göttingen, 1963. English translation by M. G. Rogers, *Yahweh War and Tribal Confederation*, Nashville and New York, 1970.

35. S. Herrmann, *Geschichte Israels in alttestamentliche Zeit*, Munich, 1973.

36. G. von Rad, 'Der Anfang der Geschichtsschreibung im Alten Israel', in *Archiv für Kulturgeschichte* 32, Weimar, 1944, pp. 1–42. English translation by E. W. T. Dicken, 'The Beginnings of Historical Writing in Ancient Israel', in *The Problem of the Hexateuch and Other Essays*, pp. 166–204.

37. R. N. Whybray, *The Succession Narrative. A Study of II Samuel: 9–20 and I Kings 1 and 2* (*SBT* Second Series 9), London, 1968.

38. E. R. Leach, 'The Legitimacy of Solomon', in *Genesis as Myth and Other Essays*, London, 1969, pp. 25–83.

39. A. Alt, *'Die Staatenbildung der Israeliten in Palestina'*, Leipzig, 1930: English translation *Essays on Old Testament History and Religion*, Oxford, 1966, pp. 185–187.

40. J. H. Grønbaek, *Die Geschichte vom Aufstieg Davids (1 Samuel: 15–2 Samuel: 5). Tradition und Komposition* (Acta Theologica Danica x), Copenhagen, 1971.

4

Interpreting the Prophets

Whilst the main thrust of the fresh critical approach to the Old Testament at the end of the nineteenth century concentrated on the Pentateuch it held the prophets to be the true creative pioneers behind Israel's faith. As a result the rather unexpected pattern of interpretation had developed in which the main achievement lay in a radical reassessment of the growth and structure of the Pentateuch, while the developments of religion which were thought to explain this growth were attributed to the prophets. Although Wellhausen saw in the Old Testament prophets the true pioneers of Israel's faith and the founders of ethical monotheism, he offered no detailed interpretation of the prophetic books in explanation of this. His major work on the prophets was a short annotated translation of the twelve minor prophets which has rightly become valued as a classic of its kind, but this on account of its textual and philological contribution rather than any broader exegetical content.

Undoubtedly Wellhausen's regard for the prophets goes back to his own highly regarded teacher Heinrich Ewald, the semitist and theologian who had seen in them inspired revolutionary spirits, who combined in their make-up both intellectual genius and irrepressible zeal for reform and spiritual renewal. Nevertheless there is force in the stricture which H. Gunkel later made, that even the great Wellhausian school, which had brought about such a far-reaching change in Old Testament studies, had done little to produce a clearer understanding of the true nature of the prophets. For this Gunkel points rather to two men: B. Duhm and G. Hölscher.[1]

B. Duhm was born in Bingum in East Friesland in 1847, and, like Wellhausen, had studied under Ewald in Göttingen where the two men became close friends. Duhm's first major work, entitled *Die Theologie der Propheten*, was published in 1875[2] and thus appeared almost contemporaneously with Wellhausen's first important essays on the composition of the Hexateuch. Like Wellhausen, Duhm accepted Graf's thesis that the Law which is now to be found in the great Priestly literary collection of legal and cultic regulations was later than the prophets. The way was thereby made free for Duhm to approach the task of interpreting the prophets on the internal evidence of the prophetic books alone, without constant reference to a complex and developed tradition of religious ideas and institutions which lay behind them.

In this light the prophets were seen to be creative innovators in the sphere of religious ideas, breaking sharply with inherited beliefs and practices, and establishing clear basic principles which afterwards became fundamental to the concepts of truth in religion. The very title of the book, *The Theology of the Prophets*, reveals much of the character of Duhm's interpretation. The foremost achievements of the prophets lay in the realm of theological ideas, and especially in the way in which they criticized and rejected the cultic practices with their half-magical assumptions with which Israel had grown up. The prophets replaced these with a religion of moral idealism. The preaching of Amos could readily be summarized by Duhm as 'ethical idealism' (p. 126), and each of the great prophets from Amos to Deutero-Isaiah, with the exception of Ezekiel whose preaching was thought not to point to a single new idea of religious or moral worth (p. 259), could be seen to have contributed towards a new ideal of religion. This ideal was essentially one of the primacy of morality in religion, with the ethicizing of the concept of holiness and a discovery of the direct relationship of the individual to God. Even though the concept of a national religion was not truly overcome in the Old Testament, it was nevertheless possible to single out Isaiah as having come to a new conception of the people of God (pp. 174f.), which was basically that of a church of the faithful. Unhesitatingly Duhm pointed to Micah 6:1–8 as 'the most important passage in the prophetic literature' (p. 183), and saw in the prophets generally a new conception of religion which made them teachers of the true religious and moral values of mankind.

While this fresh emphasis upon the moral idealism of the prophets admittedly took account of the historical context in which the prophetic preaching had been made, it regarded this context as a kind of ephemeral dress, which did not affect the lasting nature of the message brought by the prophets. This lay in the moral ideas which they expressed. W. Robertson Smith, who was himself considerably influenced by Duhm's book, could criticize it as somewhat doctrinaire,[3] and so indeed it is. Its reflection of the moral idealism of nineteenth century philosophy is palpably evident, and its attempt to present the prophets as theologians in disguise is an inadequate portrait of them, as Duhm himself afterwards realized. Nonetheless it is an exciting book, alive with a great sense of the relevance and appeal of the prophets, and full of positive ideas and interesting interpretation.

Its few strictures upon the traditional orthodoxy of conservative theologians in which the prophets were regarded as foretellers of the coming of Christ through a series of cryptic predictions are a very minor feature. In a far broader compass than Christian orthodoxy had hitherto grasped Duhm believed he could show that the prophets had prepared the way for the Christian gospel by their moral earnestness, their rejection of a religion of ritual, and their preaching of the direct relationship of each individual to God. Whatever loss was incurred by divorcing the prophets from narrow theological schemes of promise and fulfilment was more than redressed by pointing to their relevance for the moral claims of Christianity. Even more than this the prophets could be seen to belong not simply to Israel and to the Christian church, but to mankind as a whole, since their message embraced the moral and religious concerns of every man. The forceful positive note which Duhm's interpretation posed heralded a new, and more broadly based, form of apologetic which argued that we must go back to the prophets to learn from them the revelation of the moral nature of religion and the personal and ethical basis of each man's relationship to God.

Duhm's presentation of the prophets as theologians readily appears inadequate in the light of a further century of critical scholarship and examination of the prophetic books. Nevertheless it was in considerable measure this emphasis which Duhm gave to the prophets, and which he shared with Wellhausen, which has characterized much of their interpretation in the twentieth century. In essence it can be seen in retrospect to represent a substantial over-emphasis upon the originality of the contribution of the prophets, especially in the realm of ethical and religious ideas.

Duhm's work was understandably accepted and followed by many scholars as a great step forward in research, while equally understandably it inevitably aroused reaction and criticism from conservative theological circles. At first Duhm's career appeared to suffer somewhat as a consequence of such conservative reaction and he had to wait until 1889 before being elected to an ordinary professorship at Basel, where he taught until his death following a street accident in 1928.[4]

After the publication of his book on the prophetic theology, Duhm produced nothing further, not even an article, for seventeen years, until in 1892 the first edition of his Isaiah commentary appeared. The freshness of this new work, coming after a considerable interval leaves no doubt that Duhm had become conscious of the onesidedness of his earlier interpretation of the prophets, and in the intervening years he had deeply concerned himself with two fundamental features of prophecy which markedly affect the prophetic books. The first is the fact that the prophets were poets, a feature which had been recognized since the days of Robert Lowth. However it had been only partially explored, and Duhm now rediscovered it.[5] This especially affected the literary form of the prophetic books. The second feature is related to this and concerns the fact that the prophets were not primarily thinkers—either philosophers or theologians—in any conventional sense, but had received their messages in highly distinctive and emotional ecstatic experiences. In his earlier book Duhm had referred to the strange psychological manifestations of prophetic activity in visions and ecstasy, but had dismissed them as secondary. They were regarded as features which tended to disappear once the prophet had perceived the moral nature of his task.[6] In his commentary on Isaiah, however, Duhm returned to reconsider this feature and clearly recognized that the unusual psychological aspects of the prophets were neither as subordinate, nor as ephemeral, as he had at first argued. On this point his work marked a further step in the recognition of the importance of this psychological aspect for an understanding of the prophets. From this beginning it quickly became a central point of interest in the study of the prophetic books through the writings of other scholars, notably Gunkel and Hölscher.

Duhm's rediscovery of the poetic nature of prophecy enabled him to use it to provide a new aspect of criticism in his Isaiah commentary which he regarded as of paramount importance. His awareness of the metrical form of prophetic utterance made possible the use of an analysis of metre as a fundamental criterion for recognizing the division of the individual speech units. In this way it became a means for discovering and removing glosses, additions and other secondary material.

This in turn facilitated Duhm's great concern to recover the original text of the book, and through this to get back to the authentic words of the prophet himself.

While Duhm's metrical theories have called for much further investigation, and have required revision and modification, he had nevertheless established by means of it a new pattern of literary criticism for the prophetic literature. The central aim of this was to separate the 'authentic' from the 'inauthentic' material which had been added to it. In the preface to the first edition of his Isaiah commentary Duhm singled out this concern with poetic form and metre as an aid fully as valuable to the scholar as the evidence of the ancient versions. Duhm coupled this with his earlier attention to the religious ideas of the prophets, and a warm personal support for the literary-critical methods of Wellhausen with all their stylistic, historical and theological ramifications. Together they encouraged him to write a commentary in which the dominating concern was to recover what the prophet had actually said. Only on the basis of having established what this was, did Duhm feel entitled to go on to ask what was meant by it. More recent criticism would undoubtedly wish to recognize that the reverse procedure is often as important, since what a passage means will help to define the context in which it could have been uttered.

Duhm's basic arguments for separating the different sections of the book of Isaiah, especially the distinctness of the major collections in chapters 1–39, 40–55 and 56–66, have become a most important landmark in the criticism of the book. However the methods which Duhm fashioned to reach his results have probably been of greater influence upon scholarship than those results themselves. In retrospect these techniques of criticism can be seen to have been too refined, as is, for example, the case in Duhm's too sharp a separation of the Servant Songs of Deutero-Isaiah from their context. Nonetheless they have provided a necessary tool of research towards recognizing the long and complex literary history through which the material of the prophetic books has passed. In the light of further examination it can be seen that the great weakness of this approach has been its too hasty dismissal of so much material as unimportant or irrelevant simply because it could not clearly be identified as authentic to the original prophet. The purpose of such additions and their immense value for the interpretation of the prophetic books have too often been ignored.

Duhm wrote a number of other commentaries on poetic books of the Old Testament, most notably a very constructive volume on Jeremiah,[7] on Job[8] and the Psalms.[9] The Jeremiah commentary in particular marked a considerable milestone because of the large amount of secondary, non-Jeremianic, material which Duhm sought to identify and remove from the discussion of the prophet Jeremiah himself. This included a large collection of prose sermons which bear close connections with the Deuteronomic writings of the Old Testament. Whereas the poetic addresses of the main prophecies collected in chapters 1–25 were regarded by Duhm as essentially Jeremianic, the prose sermons were so different in style and thought, and so closely related to Deuteronomy, that he concluded that he must set them aside as inauthentic. The problem posed by these prose sermons has continued to be a central area in Jeremiah studies, and the insights of Duhm have undoubtedly been fundamental to subsequent researches.

Alongside of these commentaries, which Duhm clearly found to be the most congenial form of critical research into the Old Testament, he also published in 1916 a substantially revised presentation of the main religious teaching of the prophets under the title *Israels Propheten*.[10] In this he shows a much more restrained and cautious approach from that which was evident in the exciting, but admittedly very one-sided, presentation of his first book. On one major point his change of view reflects a growing uncertainty among scholars about the rightness of regarding the classical prophets from Amos onwards as the true creative geniuses of Israel's faith. Duhm now restored Moses to a place as the first of the prophets and regarded him, not as a lawgiver in any traditionally accepted sense, but as a prophetic figure to be set alongside Elijah and Elisha as forerunners of prophecy's dramatic flowering with Amos. By this change, and without conceding that the Law in any substantial sense preceded the prophets, Duhm nevertheless re-affirmed the creative role of Moses in the founding of Israel's religion.

In his studies of prophecy Duhm recognized that the poetic element in it was closely related to the elevated and excited consciousness of the prophet who believed that God was speaking through him. Accompanying this elevated consciousness he saw that the prophets had undergone strange psychological experiences of visions and auditions and had manifested a wide variety of forms of impulsive behaviour associated with a state of ecstasy.

The discovery of the unusual psychology of prophetic experience marked out the prophets as preachers and public speakers, and showed that their primary activity was at some distance from the composition of the books which now bear their names. This interest in their psychology rapidly developed into a major feature of research on the prophets in which their strangeness was viewed with a kind of romantic fascination, and their dissimilarity from conventional thinkers and theologians firmly noted. Outstanding here was the work of Gustav Hölscher, who used various of the classifications of W. Wundt's *Völkerpsychologie*[11] to arrive at a markedly different assessment of the nature of the prophets from those which looked only at their theology and religious ideas. This was in a substantial volume, published in 1914, entitled *Die Profeten. Untersuchungen zur Religionsgeschichte Israels.*[12]

Hölscher examined the various phenomena associated with ecstatic and visionary experiences: a sense of heightened awareness, loss of bodily feeling, concentration of thought, uncontrolled bodily actions, dreams, hallucinations, hypnotic visions, experiences of dumbness, amnesia and paralysis. All of these he related to specific actions designed to induce such ecstatic experience through music, dancing and various cultic and mantic rites. He went on to consider the connection which these activities bore to phenomena of prediction and of claims to see events taking place elsewhere. Aspects of these strange manifestations of prophetic and mantic activity were seen by Hölscher to be present in differing degrees in the Old Testament prophets. Of great importance to his thesis was an attempt to show that a historical and genetic connection held together the whole prophetic movement. Hence he sought to trace a recognizable origin for Israel's ecstatic prophecy through historical and racial features associated with Israel's settlement in Canaan.

He pointed to the existence of a priestly mantic movement centred on Kadesh in the southern desert where, he argued, Moses had officiated as priest. There, he claimed, Moses had certainly shared in the obtaining of oracles by means of a sacred lot. Nevertheless this was a technical and priestly activity which was to be distinguished from the oracle-giving of the free ecstatic prophets. The origin of this latter, Hölscher argued, was to be found in Syria, and behind this in Asia Minor. It had come to affect Israel after the settlement in Palestine and made its first appearance in Israel in the age of Saul. Thereafter it became an influential and dominant movement, reaching its climax in the great classical prophetic figures of the Old Testament. Using this reconstruction of the history, Hölscher argued that the Israelite nation first encountered ecstatic prophecy among the Canaanites, and had taken it over from them. In the process, however, what had originally been a strange and bizarre form of ecstatic behaviour, associated with the giving of oracles and the utterance of all kinds of threats, warnings and promises, became imbued with a new moral spirit. Thus out of an unusual, but widely known, form of religious behaviour there emerged a new, and truly revelatory, form of religion.

Hölscher's work undoubtedly marked the end of any treatment of the prophets which concerned itself solely with their religious ideas, and which, since the work of H. Ewald, had seen their main contribution to Israel's religion to lie in the realm of their interpretation, or reinterpretation, of basic religious concepts and experiences. In this regard it established an awareness that the prophets were strange and highly distinctive religious figures, who could not readily be compared to conventional thinkers and theologians. Behind such an approach there was undoubtedly an element of romanticism which saw in the strangeness of such prophetic behaviour a degree of mystery associated with a divine intrusion into human affairs. Looking back we may also note with surprise how readily psychological explanations were assumed to provide a key to understanding the nature of divine revelation with all its theological implications. We should also wish to criticize the assumption that racial and genetic lineage can explain the history and development of religious movements, especially when they contain highly distinctive ideas, such as Israelite prophecy undoubtedly did. Nevertheless the publication of Hölscher's *Die Profeten* set an end to attempts at interpreting the prophets solely in terms of their distinctive religious ideas.

The new awareness of the strangeness of much of the prophetic activity had enabled Hölscher to open up a new field of enquiry. After the publication of a historical study of the development of Israel's religion in 1922, he presented in 1923 an examination of the literary character and origin of the book of Ezekiel, which radically broke with earlier critical studies of the book.[13] These had seen a substantial literary unity in the book of Ezekiel, relatively free from the biting questions concerning the separation of authentic from inauthentic material, such as had come to characterize the books of Isaiah and Jeremiah. Even Gunkel had been able to describe Ezekiel as 'the first prophet who wrote a book'.[14] Now Hölscher felt that he possessed in his understanding of the psychology of prophetic ecstasy a key towards recovering the actual living situation in which Ezekiel's prophecy had been proclaimed. This was not in a world of quiet reflection and literary composition, but in an unusual state of heightened openness to the divine action. Hölscher himself believed that the prophets usually proclaimed their messages in an ecstatic trance-like state, in which poetry was the natural mode of expression. Only later was this original poetic utterance recorded and written down. On such a basis he separated in the book of Ezekiel the original poetic sayings of the prophet from the extensive prose discourses and compositions in the book, which he ascribed to the work of later editors. Thereby only a relatively small percentage of the extant book of Ezekiel was left to be credited to the original prophet.

This glance forward at Hölscher's later work, however, with its very radical conclusions, illustrates further the interest and value of his book of 1914. The study of Ezekiel is readily intelligible as a further application of the interest in the psychology of prophetic experience, the relationship of this to poetic speech, and the discovery that the writing down of books of prophecy represents a late stage in the history of the prophet's sayings. Hölscher's understanding of the phenomenon of prophecy was not new in its interpretative insights, but more radical in the way in which it developed and extended them.

Duhm had earlier noted the ecstatic nature of prophetic experience, and this aspect of prophecy had come to hold a special fascination for H. Gunkel. In an essay, first published in 1903 with the title 'The Mysterious Experiences of the Prophets', and later revised and printed along with three other essays on the prophets in book form in 1917,[15] Gunkel affirmed that the prophets were men of strange experiences and mysterious, often cryptic, utterance. The jacket of the little book on the prophets is illustrated with a beautiful line drawing of John the Baptist by Steinhausen in which Gunkel took special delight. It captured the sensation of wild and vigorous action, coupled with mystic rapture, which Gunkel regarded as characteristic of the Old Testament prophets. They were not theologians, nor was their concern primarily to teach new religious ideas, for they had not themselves experienced religion primarily in the world of thought. Theirs was the world of inner piety and outward activity in an intense involvement in human affairs. By examining this world, Gunkel made it clear that his foremost interest was to understand their own private spiritual experiences. Hence he saw it as the main task of scholarship to work to obtain such an understanding of the prophets' messages in their historical context which would lay bare their own souls as men rapt in communion with God.

Like Wellhausen, Gunkel believed that the prophets represented the highwater mark of Old Testament faith and religious insight. This was the central point of Israel's contact with God, and thus the fount of revelation. Yet whereas Wellhausen had spelt out the consequences of this prophetic faith primarily in terms of religious ideas, Gunkel saw it as less definable in strictly theological terms. The prophetic faith was a communion with God which could be recognized, and described, but which was much more than just a sum of doctrines and ideas.

On one very notable point Gunkel differed from Hölscher. Whereas the latter scholar had seen the psychology of ecstasy as indicative of the condition in which the prophets had delivered their sayings, Gunkel saw it rather as applicable to the situations in which they received their messages from God. For Gunkel an element of reflection, of personal choice, and of conscious skill and artistry was seen to belong to the delivery of the prophetic message. Significantly the second of the essays published by Gunkel in *Die Propheten* of 1917 was entitled 'The Politics of the Prophets'. In this study Gunkel noted the relationship between what the prophets preached and the contemporary political situation, together with the whole nexus of events in which they and their nation were caught up. Their message was concerned quite directly with their contemporary history and with assertions about the meaning of events. Nevertheless Gunkel regarded this outward world of political turmoil as a background only against which to study the inner spiritual life of the prophets.

The most important of Gunkel's contributions to the study of prophecy, however, lay not so much in his insistence upon the strangeness, and unsystematic manner, of their thinking and speaking, as in his recognition and analysis of the forms of the prophetic literature. The rediscovered awareness that the prophets were primarily preachers, and that the prophetic books had not in most cases been written and composed by the prophets themselves, indicated that the original forms of prophecy must have been spoken forms. Gunkel's research into this subject fell into two main parts, the first of which was to seek to discover and classify the types of speech employed by the prophets themselves. The second was to learn from this the processes of development which had led to the compilation of our extant prophetic books. As in the case of his pioneering work on the stories of Genesis, Gunkel used these insights to establish the main lines of form-critical and traditio-historical study of the prophetic literature.

Already as early as 1893 Gunkel had hinted at a fresh literary approach to the prophets in an essay on Nahum 1.[16] This, he had argued, was not a genuine prophetic vision at all, but a post-prophetic psalm. Further Gunkel's essay on 'The Mysterious Experiences of the

Prophets', first published in 1903, pointed to a recognition that the prophets had primarily been speakers, and that it is only as a result of a subsequent literary development that their words had been recorded into books.

The most substantial of Gunkel's pioneering studies on the form-critical analysis of the prophets is to be found in the introduction which he contributed to Hans Schmidt's translation and brief commentary on the prophets for the comprehensive work *Die Schriften des Alten Testaments* (Band II. 2, Göttingen, 1915; second edition 1923). This introduction was originally to have been written by Hans Schmidt himself, a pupil of Gunkel's, but the advent of the First World War and Schmidt's departure into the German army led him to request Gunkel to write it.[17] In it Gunkel gives an outline history of the Near East during the years of the great prophets and offers afresh his study of the mysterious nature of the prophetic experiences. In a third chapter he goes on to deal with the prophets as writers and poets, and it is here that his observations on the forms of prophetic speech appear. A briefer presentation of these views was subsequently published as the fourth chapter of the book *Die Propheten* of 1917.

Gunkel's starting point for an analysis of the speech-forms of prophecy, which, he strongly urged, were not to be reduced to any one system because of the considerable developments that had taken place in the course of time, was found in the ecstatic nature of prophetic experience and the oracular nature of speech that was consonant with this. The prophets had originally received their messages through unusual experiences of visions and auditions in which key features were often mysterious and obscure. The natural literary counterpart to the vision was a brief narrative account in which the contents of the vision were described. In regard to auditions, however, Gunkel was of the opinion that the messages they contained were primarily made up of terse, and sometimes cryptic, sayings. So the original records of prophetic sayings would have been correspondingly brief. Out of these short sayings much larger units and compositions were developed in which a whole range of speech forms found employment. In this way promises, threats, admonitions, warnings, hymns, laments, liturgies and allegories all became established forms of speech which the prophets employed to develop and expound their messages. This, however, still left open the question of which forms were basic to prophetic speech. To this Gunkel responded by pointing to threats and promises, the predictions of woe or of deliverance and renewal, as fundamental. In its purest form Gunkel suggested that this preaching was to be seen in the oracles against foreign nations, although, as W. Klatt points out,[18] he certainly did not mean to deny that it was also to be seen as basic in the prophecies addressed to Israel. Here, however, Gunkel believed that the need to bring about an understanding and acceptance of such threats and promises on the part of the prophet's hearers had led to a process of development in which an extensive range of supporting material found employment.

Gunkel saw this development as having led to a supplementation of the simple threat by invective in which the reasons for the coming disaster were set out. For this reason Gunkel regarded the increasingly moral concern of prophecy as having brought about a considerable change in its form. The simple oracular threat more and more fell into the background behind the invective which explained the divine necessity of coming disaster. In course of time the invective came to take precedence over the threat, and the major task of the prophets came to be the uncovering of their people's sin. Thereby the invective assumed a quite independent place within prophecy, and took on the character of a new and distinctive prophetic form. In line with this development Gunkel saw the ecstatic side of prophecy, and the purely oracular and predictive features which were associated with it, as declining in significance as the prophetic ideas of God, and of his moral government of the world, came into the forefront. It was on this account that Gunkel believed that the prophetic literature represented the highpoint of the literary development of Israel.

In this analysis, in which Gunkel for the first time drew serious attention to the types (*Gattungen*) of prophetic speech, he made a most useful distinction between those forms which were primary and peculiar to the prophets, and those which had only been taken over by them in a secondary way. Among these latter he listed such religious types as songs of rejoicing, mocking songs, laments, pilgrimage songs, as well as the profane types of drinking songs, lovesongs and the like. The recognition of the primary types brought out very clearly the element of prediction which lay at the heart of prophecy, but the use by the prophets of lyric and profane forms also betrayed a most important development. These forms, Gunkel argued, were older than prophecy and had been taken up into it. Yet they had in turn been influenced and remoulded by it so that the later religious lyric forms in Israel became deeply imbued with the prophetic spirit. Thus, as Gunkel's studies of the Psalms endeavoured to show, this mutual interaction between prophecy and lyric psalmody left a profound mark upon Israel's literary development. The fuller discussion of this belongs to the history of the interpretation of the psalms.

Gunkel's recognition of the fundamental place of prediction within prophecy soon found further corroboration in a study of L. Köhler of the form and style of prophetic language in Deutero-Isaiah.[19] Köhler recognized that the frequently recurring formula 'Thus says Yahweh', or more properly 'Thus has Yahweh said', was parallel to the formula by which a messenger announced the contents of the message which had been entrusted to him (cf. Genesis 32: 3–5). By this formula the prophet was putting himself in the position of a messenger from Yahweh, announcing his future plans and intentions regarding his people. Although in its origin this was a profane, or non-religious form, it had evidently become a most important speech-form among the prophets, as is shown by their widespread use of it.

The further elaboration at the hands of a large number of scholars of the various speech-forms to be found in prophecy need not be listed in detail here. The fundamental recognition that certain forms, whatever their original setting, had come to be peculiarly linked with prophecy, and thus belonged to its expression and its literary development, whilst others were more consciously profane forms which the prophets employed chiefly for their verbal and stylistic effect has been of considerable significance. In later researches the individual preferences which prophets have been thought to show in their use of forms of a particular type have been used to try to establish some indication of the religious background of the prophet himself, and to serve as a pointer to the sources of ideas and images used in his preaching. Such analyses have sometimes concentrated rather heavily upon endeavouring to show the connections of certain prophets with the cultus which extended very considerably the interest of Gunkel himself in this sphere.

The fuller exploration of this field of study is to be found in the writings of S. Mowinckel, who paid special attention to the ways in which the prophetic books demonstrated the use which the prophets made of types of speech, ideas and themes drawn from the cult. Mowinckel's debt to Gunkel is both strongly admitted and clearly evident in a number of writings. As early as 1914 he published a study of the sources and composition of the book of Jeremiah which fully illustrates this.[20]

In 1901, in his commentary on Jeremiah, Duhm had demonstrated that the affinities of large sections of Jeremiah with the thought, language and style of Deuteronomy occurred in material which could be seen to be secondary on account of its prose form, the true language of prophecy being poetry. At the outset of his study Mowinckel points out what he regards as two fundamental errors in the current criticism of the prophetic literature, and by this there can be no doubt that he was primarily referring to the work of Duhm, especially in regard to the latter's commentary on Jeremiah. The first of these criticisms is of a failure to grasp the true nature and structure of the prophetic books by looking for some logical order in the arrangement of the material. The second is related to this and concerned an over pre-occupation with distinctions between authentic and inauthentic material.

From this starting point Mowinckel proceeded to argue that, as Gunkel had shown, the basic form of prophetic speech was that of an oracular utterance, couched in poetry, and usually making free use of the 'I' form in which God spoke directly through the prophet. This type of poetic material was to be found extensively within Jeremiah 1–25, and was labelled by Mowinckel source A. Alongside this was a series of historical narratives (the so-called Baruch Biography), which had as their main purpose the recording of the occasions of memorable sayings (source B). The third class of material (source C) consisted of a number of prose sermons scattered throughout the book, and clearly showing signs of connection with Deuteronomy, as Duhm had argued. The fourth class of material (source D) consisted of hopeful prophecies contained in chapters 30–31.

Only after having classified the material in this way did Mowinckel regard it as appropriate to raise the question of the authenticity of the material, since the first need was to understand how these different types of material were related to the preaching of Jeremiah. In a later work dealing with the questions of the way in which the original preaching of the prophets was related to the written tradition which preserved this message, Mowinckel returned to these issues.[21] So far as his own earlier study of Jeremiah was concerned he affirmed that the main way in which he wished to modify his earlier conclusions was in noting more fully the links between the various classes of tradition material with a view to recognizing their interrelationships.[22]

One of the most far-reaching aspects of Mowinckel's development of Gunkel's method of *Gattungsgeschichte* in relation to the prophetic books concerned the relationship between prophecy and the cultus. This became a very significant aspect of the form criticism of the Psalter. The awareness that some of the forms of composition which are to be found in the Psalter are also to be found in prophecy had come to the fore even before Gunkel himself turned his attention directly to the classification of the various psalm types. This is well shown by Gunkel's early essay on Nahum 1. When looking at the Psalms more directly, however, the whole field of study grew in scope and importance very considerably. Not only was Gunkel able to suggest that certain prophecies made use of liturgical forms otherwise found in the Psalter, but he also argued extensively that many of the most central aspects of the development of psalmody in Israel could only be explained by postulating the influence of prophecy on the Psalms, in its ideas as well as its more formal features. Hence we could trace liturgical forms in prophecy and also see evidence of prophetic preaching in the Psalter.[23]

The major problems which these insights raised were those of establishing some kind of chronology of development so that we might see which had influenced which, and in what way. Thus we can find evidence in prophecy, as for example in Jeremiah 14: 17–22, of a communal act of lamentation appropriate to a national day of penitence and prayer. In this case the divine response to this act of communal penitence was expressed through the prophet by a word of admonition from God, although on another occasion we can readily assume that it could have been through a prophetic message of assurance. Gunkel himself recognized that this word of God's answer to the people's appeal must have been related in some way to the liturgical forms of the cult in which a priest, or some such figure, gave answer on God's behalf to the assembled worshippers. Mowinckel took up this point and especially challenged Gunkel for not being willing to carry the implications of these insights through to their logical conclusion:

> Gunkel had raised here an idea that is fruitful in several directions, but immediately let it go again without pressing on to a clear understanding which corresponds to the whole reality. He could have had here an Ariadne thread of psalm exegesis, but rejected it because Wellhausen—Stade—Smend were still too strongly in him.[24]

In examining the progress of psalm criticism we can see the way in which Mowinckel used this new knowledge to recover an understanding of the cultic prophecy which underlies a number of psalms. So far as the prophetic literature was directly concerned Mowinckel pointed to one book in particular, that of Habakkuk, as an example of the kind of cultic prophecy he was concerned with. Here Habakkuk 1–2 takes the form of a cultic lament, expressing national distress and appealing to God to answer the people's cry for help. Habakkuk 3 correspondingly is a psalm in which assurance of this divine help is provided. Mowinckel further pointed to Joel 1–2 as an illustration of a similar example of a cultic lament in prophecy, noting that Gunkel had already observed this fact.

Mowinckel's next major contribution to the study of the prophetic literature turned to a different subject, but carried the insights already gained into the relationship between psalmody and prophecy a stage further. This was concerned with the composition of the book of Isaiah, and in it Mowinckel pointed to the importance of the part played in its composition by a band of Isaianic disciples.[25] The many points of connection in thought and language between the prophecies of Isaiah, especially in Isaiah 1–12, and the Psalter pointed to a common connection with the Jerusalem cultus. Could this not then be best explained by a recognition of a link between the prophetic disciples of Isaiah mentioned in Isaiah 8:16 and the temple prophets of Jerusalem? If this was the case then the activities of these same temple prophets must provide the explanation for the links between Isaiah and Micah, especially in the picture of an eschatological pilgrimage to Mount Zion affirmed in Micah 4:1–4 and Isaiah 2:2–4. But as a result of Mowinckel's concern with the annual celebration of a Festival of Yahweh's Enthronement in Jerusalem, the work of these same Jerusalem temple prophets was also found in other parts of the Old Testament, notably the Decalogue and the book of Deuteronomy. By noting these connections the wide influences of elements associated with the Jerusalem temple cult were linked by Mowinckel with the prophetic preaching of Isaiah and the circles of tradents who had been responsible for the initial formation of the book which carries his name.

In retrospect it was no doubt unfortunate that Mowinckel drew most attention in his presentation to the claim that the Jerusalem temple prophets were to be regarded as the disciples of Isaiah. Hence it is not surprising that in his later studies he did not return to this particular hypothesis. What he had achieved, however, in a rather over-pressed argument, was a demonstration that there were many important points of connection in thought, language and speech-form, between the prophetic books of Isaiah, Micah, Habakkuk and Nahum on the one hand and the Psalter and 'legal' material of the Decalogue and the book of Deuteronomy on the other. The real common element which Mowinckel had spotted was the influence of the Jerusalem temple cult, not that of the otherwise vague and little known disciples of Isaiah.

Mowinckel's understanding of the prophetic books worked on the assumption that the prophet's original words had been memorized and handed on by groups of disciples who exercised a formative role in the compilation of the prophetic books which we now have. Hence the belief in the existence of circles of disciples, or 'schools' of the great prophetic leaders was taken to be an important key to understanding how our prophetic books had come into existence. Such a view carried with it the belief in a period of oral transmission during which the prophet's original words had been supplemented and 'developed' in the light of events and needs subsequent to his preaching.

This contrasted with the view that individual sayings of the prophets would have been written down at a very early stage, perhaps roughly scratched on potsherds, and brought together into collections somewhat later. Thus, while the production of a 'book' was a relatively late stage in the process of transmitting the prophet's words, some of them would have been put into writing quite early. On such a view it was legitimate to attempt to distinguish clearly between the 'authentic' material which had derived from the prophet, and the 'inauthentic' sayings which had not originally come from him.

We have already noted that Mowinckel was opposed to such a sharp demarcation in his assessment of the sources of the book of Jeremiah, because it paid too little attention to the different types of material preserved in the book. By pointing to the prophet's disciples as the effective authors of the book of sayings attributed to him, Mowinckel argued that the material collected in such a book was related in varying degrees of closeness to what the prophet had actually said. Inevitably some degree of interpretation, and even of later re-application, of the prophecies became incorporated into the book. These questions were taken up afresh and reconsidered by Mowinckel in 1946 in a book *Prophecy and Tradition*[26].

Before this time, however, the consequences of a period of oral transmission of the prophets' words before the compilation of the books which now bear their names was raised in a very prominent way by the Swedish scholar H.S. Nyberg. This distinguished Semitist from Uppsala published a short study of the book of Hosea in 1935,[27] in which he argued that many of the problems of the text of Hosea must be studied in the light of the general assumption that all prophecy was originally transmitted orally. In his view the written Old Testament was, throughout, a post-exilic creation since early communities only resorted to the preservation of their religious traditions in writing when they felt them to be threatened in some way. For Israel this threat, with its putting in jeopardy of the continuity of normal religious life and activity, had been brought about by the Babylonian exile. Thus he argued that in the case of the prophet Hosea, his preaching in the middle of the eighth century had been preserved orally by a school of tradents, or disciples, and that it could not be regarded as having been committed to writing until much later.

This general understanding of the importance of oral transmission of sacred texts in ancient Israel was taken up energetically by Nyberg's pupil I. Engnell, who applied it to Hosea and to the prophetic books generally.[28] In the case of Hosea the effects of such a view become most marked, since it encouraged Engnell to discount the widely held view that the book had undergone a considerable amount of editing at the hands of Judean scribes. Engnell, however, argued that this Judean element must be treated as belonging to the book as we have it and taken as expressive of Hosea's preaching. To Engnell the very idea that we can now, by literary-critical methods, sort out the genuine from the non-genuine sayings of any prophet was regarded as totally false. What we have is the written deposit of what men remembered of the prophets' preaching, as they had taught it and handed it on over a long period. To some extent Mowinckel also shared in such a view, as also did his pupil Harris Birkeland, who endeavoured to show the importance of such oral transmission for an understanding of prophecy.[29]

G. Widengren, another of Nyberg's pupils from Uppsala, argued on a more cautious note that we must not come too hastily to the conclusion that all prophecy was originally transmitted orally, and that prophetic books are necessarily a late phenomenon.[30] By adducing analogies from comparable situations in Islamic tradition Widengren argued that in some cases religious texts, including prophecies, may be written down from the beginning. We must therefore allow that some prophecies may have been written almost from the time of their utterance, and that both oral and written transmission can exist side by side in religious communities.

Certainly for a time the hypothesis of a relatively long period of oral transmission within a circle of prophetic disciples came to dominate the study of the prophetic texts. In many respects its value has remained as a working hypothesis, although its importance has undoubtedly suffered from exaggeration. That all prophets formed circles of disciples has not been proven, and the almost total silence about them and their activities in the prophetic books themselves, counsels further caution. More directly too, the idea that it is a fruitless quest to attempt to sift the prophetic sayings in order to remove later additions and glosses is something of a counsel of despair. The very strength of the study of the prophetic books since the work of Duhm has been its growing skill in achieving this. However what such study has increasingly shown is that the categories of 'genuine' and 'non-genuine' are often not appropriate for a proper description of the material to which they are applied. So often what we are faced with in the prophetic books are sayings of the prophets which have been developed and supplemented in a very meaningful way. As a result a proper study of the redactional interests and intentions displayed by the completed text has become a major key towards obtaining an understanding of how the prophet's original sayings were understood and applied. In other cases, as for example in that of the book of Jeremiah, it is rather jumping to conclusions to assume that the process of editing which the book displays, and the supplementation of the original Jeremianic prophecies by later additions, must be ascribed to a circle of the prophet's disciples.

Gunkel's recognition that certain prophecies showed a liturgical form, and may be understood as prophetic adaptations of cultic sayings and activities, pointed to a possible source in the cult of various ideas and images used by the prophets. Such a claim was taken up and developed extensively by Mowinckel in his studies of the Psalter, and led him to postulate the existence of cult-prophets, who must be regarded as professional members of the staffs of the great sanctuaries of Israel. Thus, as we have seen, in his study of the book of Isaiah, Mowinckel pointed to a large number of features in the prophecies which can best be accounted for on the assumption that they have been drawn from the Zion temple prophets. In his study of the elements in the Psalter which reflect this cult prophecy Mowinckel pointed to the Old Testament books of Joel, Nahum and Habakkuk as examples of it in prophetic collections. This suggestion was taken up by various scholars in studies devoted to these books. The French scholar P. Humbert examined the book of Habakkuk[31] and found it to be a liturgy of the kind that Mowinckel had suggested. Similarly the Swedish scholar A. Haldar[32] devoted his attention to this book with comparable results, while Mowinckel's own pupil A. S. Kapelrud turned his attention to the book of Joel.[33] In all these cases the connection between the prophecy and the cult was seen to extend far beyond the use of liturgical forms and language. The ideas and word-pictures used by these cult-prophets were interpreted as drawn from themes and mythological images which had their original setting in the cult. The descriptions of battle and invading forces were regarded as stereotyped mythological scenes, rather than as references to specific historical powers. As a result of these studies the *gattungsgeschichtliche* method initiated by Gunkel was carried very much further into the realm of traditio-history and used as a tool by which the very content of prophetic sayings could be interpreted and explained.

In a way that is often difficult to appreciate fully in retrospect the newer picture of prophecy which was emerging showed how extensively many prophetic sayings had made use of earlier traditions. For the most part these were regarded as having had their original setting in Israel's cult. Mowinckel's study of Isaiah contributed further to such a method of interpretation by its claim to see in the book the themes and ideas of the Jerusalem temple worship, which Mowinckel explained as a consequence of the fact that the prophet's disciples formed the circle of temple prophets there. In a study which looked in the same direction, I. Engnell argued that the account of Isaiah's call bore a large number of traces of its original liturgical setting in the Jerusalem temple worship, showing still further the extent of the prophet's dependence on earlier cultic tradition.[34] All of this contrasted sharply with the earlier critical view that the prophets were the real originators of the main religious and theological ideas of the Old Testament, which had only subsequently been taken over into the cult and the piety of the psalmists. The method of traditio-history was being applied to the prophets in a quite extensive way and coming up with somewhat surprising results. That all of these pre-prophetic 'traditions' were traced to the cult, with the result that the prophets were themselves being made to appear more and more as the spokesmen of the cult, was clearly a one-sided reaction to the older critical view.

In Germany this traditio-historical approach to the prophets was followed up by a considerable number of scholars in the early 1950's in which the dependence of the prophets on earlier traditions was stressed. In passage after passage traces were found of the use of liturgies, hymns and ritual practices. In a very imposing theological treatment of the prophets G. von Rad developed this method of study to use it as a key to the understanding of the theological message proclaimed by them.[35] In his treatment von Rad was concerned not so much directly with the cultic forms and language for themselves, but with the particular historical traditions which he traced back to separate cult centres. Each prophet was seen to be the heir of a particular understanding of his people's past as a consequence of the traditions which had been mediated to him by the cult centre which formed his background. In this way the dependence of Hosea upon the traditions of North Israel, and the impact exerted upon Isaiah by traditions of Mount Zion and the Jerusalem temple, became key features in obtaining an understanding of the theological significance of what the prophet had said. Most prominent in this regard was the way in which these older, locally centred, historical traditions provided a clue to interpreting the way in which each prophet outlined his own eschatological picture of Yahweh's future plans for his people. The prophetic eschatology was seen to be heavily coloured by the earlier accounts of Yahweh's saving work on his people's behalf and a kind of 'typology' created in which the old saving actions of God were used to provide a picture, and thereby to give content, to the announcements of the coming eschatological renewal of his people.

Alongside this very distinctive traditio-historical approach to prophecy by G. von Rad we must set the work of his successor as Professor of Old Testament at Heidelberg, H. W. Wolff. This scholar fully accepted the validity of the traditio-historical method of analysing the prophetic books, and offered several valuable studies along these lines. In the case of the prophet Hosea, Wolff devoted a widely acclaimed essay to the examination of the prophet's spiritual background, and argued that it was to be found in the cultic traditions of Northern Israel, where circles of Levites kept alive many of the historic traditions and ideas of the Yahwistic faith.[36] This claim became an important factor in the interpretation of Hosea, as Wolff demonstrated in his commentary on the book.[37] When he turned to the prophet Amos, however, Wolff became very critical of the numerous attempts which had been made to trace the influence of various liturgical forms and cultic themes and ideas in the preaching of this prophet.[38] Their limitations and deficiencies led Wolff to question whether scholars had been right to look to the cult so extensively in explanation of the particular spiritual world of Amos. A fresh examination of several passages in the book led him to look in a very different direction. This was to the traditions of wisdom, and more specifically to the old clan wisdom of Israel, which was to be differentiated from the more sophisticated court wisdom which is well represented in our extant book of Proverbs. Thus what was striking about Amos, in Wolff's view, was not his dependence on the traditions and ideas of the cult, but his remarkable freedom from them. In his home in Tekoa Amos had grown up in a locality where the strongly moral and didactic concerns of clan life had been retained in the face of the growing urbanization of Israel, with its gradual breaking up of the older clan-centred life, its special values and ideals. In support of such a thesis Wolff pointed to the use by the prophet of several speech-forms which could be regarded as peculiar to wisdom on account of their

71

didactic character. He linked this with the presence of certain wisdom ideas, and the use of distinctive wisdom terminology by the prophet.

Such a changed understanding of the kind of tradition which could be regarded as underlying a prophet's preaching was obviously capable of being explored elsewhere than in Amos, and mention may here be made of its application to the study of the prophecies of Isaiah of Jerusalem.[39] By such a procedure the traditio-historical method of study could be regarded as capable of looking at the same material twice and coming up with two surprisingly different results. Valid as this is as a measure of criticism for certain extreme positions, it is unfair to regard it as typical of the method as a whole. It has brought to the study of the prophets a remarkably fresh point of view, and has further challenged the assumption that large parts of the prophetic books are made up of prophecies which have been added to the original prophet's words long after his death, and with little regard for what he had actually said. It has shown that a prophet was capable of using all kinds of allusive and cryptic sayings, drawing images sometimes from the cult and sometimes from elsewhere, such as familiar myths and legends, in presenting his message. The historical situation in which the prophet preached did not preclude his using the language and ideas of far older times.

In the interval between the publication of Wolff's study of the background of Amos and the appearance of his full commentary on the whole book it is evident that new interests and aspects of it had attracted his attention.[40] In turning from a concern to uncover the background of ideas and speech-forms which the prophet had used, to consider the final form of the book itself, Wolff pointed to the presence of an editorial framework into which the prophet's preaching had been set. That Amos, in common with other prophetic books, contained a certain amount of secondary material had long been recognized. Wolff was now concerned to identify its character and to discern what light it shed upon the interpretation of the book as a whole. His attention was drawn to its distinctively Deuteronomic character, which pointed to some connection with Josiah's reform. From this Wolff was led by a number of clues to suggest that Amos's forewarnings of disaster to the Northern Kingdom of Israel, and especially to its leading sanctuary at Bethel, had taken on a deep significance for the Deuteronomic movement. By this means Wolff pointed to a very pertinent connection between the redaction of the book of Amos and other Deuteronomic literature. This displayed a very different interest in the 'secondary' material in Amos from the earlier critics, whose main concern after identifying it had been to set it aside. Wolff now perceived that it held vitally important evidence to show us how Amos's preaching had been understood, and how its fulfilment had been looked for in events.

Such a growing concern with the history of the redaction of the prophetic books marked a further extension of Gunkel's *gattungsgeschichtliche* method, with its concern to classify the nature of the various types of material preserved in the prophetic books. The very structure of the larger written units, often with baffling alternations between threats and promises, was not an accidental production, but must have arisen in order to fulfil some significant purpose. This redactional history, through which not only Amos, but all of the prophetic books had passed, offered a valuable key towards gaining an understanding of the people and purposes which have influenced the preservation of the prophets' words. In a similar fashion the Deuteronomic material in the book of Jeremiah, which the researches of Duhm and Mowinckel had long ago uncovered, could be seen in a more constructive light as a witness to the way in which Jeremiah's preaching had been interpreted and developed in the years after his preaching activity had ceased. This material shows how the tradition of Jeremiah's preaching was held in esteem by circles of the Deuteronomic movement, and how that movement came to attach very great importance to Jeremiah's message of hope which they re-interpreted in their own distinctively theological way.

So far as the book of Ezekiel is concerned the earlier attempts, which began with the work of Hölscher, to isolate the original kernel of the prophet's preaching from an overlay of later additions and interpretations has undergone a radical re-assessment and revision. Above all in the massive commentary by W. Zimmerli,[41] it has become clear that the present book of Ezekiel is not a composition written by the prophet himself, but does, as Hölscher and others argued, contain a great deal of material which was neither written, nor spoken, by Ezekiel. Yet such material is not unrelated to Ezekiel's preaching since it emanates almost entirely from a circle of the prophet's disciples who have taken up, developed and re-applied the prophet's original words. In some cases material of this kind may have come from the prophet himself who supplemented and revised earlier prophecies in the light of the fall of Jerusalem in 587 BC. What we are faced with here is not a division between 'authentic' and 'inauthentic' material, but a living tradition of interpretation which both preserved the prophet's preaching and interpreted it in the light of events and situations which were understood as its fulfilment.

Such redaction-critical approaches to the prophetic books must be seen as an extension and development of the earlier stages of literary criticism and traditio-historical investigation. To contrast the methods with each other as representative of totally different approaches, as has occasionally been done, would be a false exaltation of one method over the others, and a failure to grasp the validity of the questions which each method has been developed to answer. The formation of our extant prophetic literature has been a long and complex process, and in order to interpret the prophets it is necessary to inquire into this process as fully as possible. The reader who comes to the prophets from the New Testament is made to realize immediately that prophecy does not have only one interpretation; instead it acquired in Israel, and later in Judaism, a complex significance as a witness to the promises and purposes of God with his people. In order to understand these it is important to learn both what the prophets said, and what their words were believed to mean.

1. H. Gunkel, *Die Propheten*, Göttingen, 1917, pp. 2–3.
2. B. Duhm, *Die Theologie der Propheten*, Bonn, 1875.
3. W. Robertson Smith, *The Prophets of Israel*, p. 1vii.
4. A brief memoir of Duhm by W. Baumgartner is given in the fifth edition of his commentary on Isaiah; *Das Buch Jesaja*, fifth edition, Göttingen, 1968, pp. V–XIII.
5. Duhm was not, of course, the first to recognize metrical features in Hebrew poetry. In 1882 K. Budde had pointed to the Kinah metre of the lament in 'Das hebräische Klagelied' in *ZAW* 2 (1882), pp. 1–52.
6. B. Duhm, *Die Theologie der Propheten*, pp. 86ff.
7. B. Duhm, *Das Buch Jeremia* (*KHAT* XI), Tübingen—Leipzig, 1901.
8. B. Duhm, *Das Buch Hiob* (*KHAT* XVI), Freiburg, 1897.
9. B. Duhm, *Psalmen* (*KHAT* XIV), Freiburg, 1899, second edition 1922.
10. B. Duhm, *Israels Propheten*, Tübingen, 1916, second edition 1922.
11. W. Wundt, *Völkerpsychologie. Eine Untersuchung der Entwicklungsgesetze von Sprache, Mythus und Sitte*, Leipzig, 1900. A useful outline of Wundt's ideas is provided in English in his *Elements of Folk Psychology. Outlines of a Psychological History of the Development of Mankind*, English translation by E. L. Schaub, London, 1916.
12. Leipzig, 1914.
13. G. Hölscher, *Hesekiel. Der Dichter und das Buch*, *BZAW* 39, Giessen, 1924.
14. H. Gunkel, 'Die Israelitische Literatur', p. 82.
15. H. Gunkel, *Die Propheten*, pp. 1–31.
16. H. Gunkel, 'Nahum 1' in *ZAW* 13 (1893), pp. 223–244.
17. The preface to the first edition, written in October 1914 by Hans Schmidt, is a most revealing document of contemporary thought and attitudes in

Germany regarding the war. Hans Schmidt, as a serving officer in the German army, expresses vividly his feelings on advancing towards the Russian front.

18. W. Klatt, *Hermann Gunkel*, p. 215; cf. *Die Propheten*, p. 125.
19. L. Köhler, *Deuterojesaja (Jesaja xl–lv) stilkritisch untersucht* (*BZAW* 37), Giessen, 1923.
20. S. Mowinckel, *Zur Komposition des Buches Jeremia*, Oslo, 1914.
21. S. Mowinckel, *Prophecy and Tradition. The Prophetic Books in the Light of the Growth and History of the Tradition*, Oslo, 1946.
22. S. Mowinckel, *Prophecy and Tradition*, pp. 62 ff.
23. H. Gunkel, article 'Psalmen' in *Die Religion in Geschichte und Gegenwart*, Bd. IV, first edition 1913; second edition 1927; English translation as *The Psalms* (Facet Books), Philadelphia, 1967, especially p. 31.
24. S. Mowinckel, *Psalmenstudien III. Kultprophetie und prophetische Psalmen*, Oslo, 1921–4; reprinted 1961, p. 2.
25. S. Mowinckel, *Jesaja-Disiplene. Profetien frå Jesaja til Jeremia*, Oslo, 1926.
26. S. Mowinckel, *Prophecy and Tradition*, Oslo, 1946.
27. H. S. Nyberg, *Studien zum Hoseabuche*, Uppsala, 1935.
28. A convenient summary of Engnell's understanding of the structure of the prophetic books for the English reader is to be found in *Critical Essays on the Old Testament*, London, 1970, pp. 123–179.
29. H. Birkeland, *Zum Hebräischen Traditionswesen. Die Komposition der prophetischen Bücher des Alten Testaments*, Oslo, 1938.
30. G. Widengren, *Literary and Psychological Aspects of the Hebrew Prophets*, Uppsala, 1948.
31. P. Humbert, *Problèmes du livre d'Habacuc*, Neuchâtel, 1944. Humbert had earlier looked at the prophecies of Nahum from this perspective; 'Le problème du livre de Nahoum', in *Revue d'histoire et de philosophie religieuse* 12 (1932), pp. 1–15.
32. A. Haldar, *Studies in the Book of Nahum*, Uppsala, 1947.
33. A. S. Kapelrud, *Joel Studies*, Oslo, 1948.
34. I. Engnell, *The Call of Isaiah. An Exegetical and Comparative*, Uppsala and Leipzig, 1949.
35. G. von Rad, *Theologie des Alten Testaments, Bd. II. Die Theologie der prophetischen Überlieferungen Israels*, Munich, 1960. English translation by D. M. G. Stalker as *Old Testament Theology*, Vol. 2, Edinburgh and London, 1965.
36. H. W. Wolff, 'Hoseas geistige Heimat' *Th.Z* 81 (1956), cols. 83–94 (= *Geschichte Studien zum Alten Testament*, in *Th.B.* 22, Neukirchen, 1964, pp. 232–250).
37. H. W. Wolff, *Hosea* (*BKAT* XIV), second edition, Neukirchen, 1965.
38. H. W. Wolff, *Amos geistige Heimat* (*WMANT* 18), Neukirchen, 1964. English translation by F. R. McCurley, *Amos the Prophet. The Man and His Background*, Philadelphia, 1973.
39. So J. W. Whedbee, *Isaiah and Wisdom*, New York and Nashville, 1971.
40. H. W. Wolff, *Joel-Amos* (*BKAT* XIV), Neukirchen 1963–9.
41. W. Zimmerli, *Ezechiel* (*BKAT* XIII), 2 vols. Neukirchen, 1955–69.

5

Interpreting the Psalms

The initial impact of a historico-critical approach to the Psalter was to produce a considerable variety of views regarding its age and character. In all respects the rejection of Davidic authorship for the Psalms, with the occasional admission of a few possible exceptions, left scholarship open to find a new place for them in the development of Israel's religion. Yet, as many scholars quickly recognized, the contents of individual psalms provided little in the way of clear indication as to the situations in which they had been composed. Furthermore the titles of the psalms, once the ascription of authorship was set aside, offered very little assistance in filling the gap. Those titles which ascribe certain psalms to particular events in David's life were rightly seen to be later additions, and to be unconfirmed by any comparable detailed historical reference in the psalm itself.

Thus, although a number of broad generalizations became current in regard to the age of the psalms, the wide divergencies in the opinions of scholars illustrated the fact that the brilliant reconstruction of the history of Israel's religion achieved by Wellhausen and others had not, thus far, been able to provide a satisfactory basis for interpreting them. The reasons for this must lie in the fact that what literary criticism had achieved was a workable and coherent picture of the history and development of Israel's religious institutions. As regards the more inward and personal side of this religious life it had secured little in the way of firm pointers to the chronology and development of Israel's piety, with its own special movements, attitudes and aims. As a result assertions about this piety were concerned primarily with broad assertions regarding the development and progress of religion from the outward forms of cult and ritual to the more inward expressions of spirituality and devotion such as are to be found in the Psalter. On the basis of these certain general categorizations became established, such as that the Psalter was 'the hymn-book of the second temple', and that in it were to be found the inner spiritual manifestations of the devotion which emerged from earlier cultic practice. The main lines of interpretation worked on the assumption, already suggested by the psalm titles, that they were written out of the personal experience of pious Israelites and that they therefore contained an element of individual, and even autobiographical, spiritual reflection.

Three main questions occupied interpreters. The first concerned the age of Israel's religious development to which the psalms in general should be ascribed. For this purpose one age in particular became a central point of reference, and this was that of the Maccabean Revolt in the second century BC. Already several earlier scholars and critics had suggested a date for the psalms in this period,[1] and J. Olshausen (1800–1882) developed such a view in a commentary.[2] Although Wellhausen does not appear generally to have been in favour of so late a date for most of the Psalter,[3] the religion and faith expressed in the psalms does not loom very prominently in his writings. His main contribution to the book is a critical edition of the Hebrew text for which he supplied notes,[4] which are almost entirely of a textual and grammatical nature.

It was left to B. Duhm, in a commentary on the Psalms published in 1899,[5] to elaborate, and to endeavour to substantiate, the case for ascribing the majority of the Psalter to the Maccabean age. Duhm denied categorically that any unprejudiced critic could arrive at the conclusion that any psalms at all derived from the pre-exilic age. He was prepared to admit that a few of them may have arisen from as early a time as the Persian period and that Psalm 137 was composed in the Babylonian exile. By far the great majority, however, he firmly placed in the second and first centuries BC. Thus he was able to see reflected in these psalms the inter-party conflicts of the first century BC and the distinctive personal piety of the Pharisaic movement.

Three main features served to suggest such a late date for a great many psalms. First, the emphasis upon a very personal and individual relationship to God was believed to reflect the freeing of religion from cultic institutions and rites, a movement which was thought to have emerged only late in the Old Testament period, after the exile when the message of the prophets had sunk deep into Israel's consciousness. Secondly, the repeated note of conflict and the frequent references to the sufferings of the psalmists at the hands of violent and godless men were taken to reflect the situation which arose in Judah in the last pre-Christian centuries. Those who were loyal to Yahweh were the poor and struggling Jews who chafed against the oppressions of the wealthy landowners who held the reins of political power and who corrupted the priesthood and religious leadership. The psalm writers were believed in large measure to be representative of the more pious communities who formed the groups of Hasidim in the time of the popular rising against Antiochus Epiphanes in the second century BC, and who later emerged as the party of the Pharisees. A third feature which was taken to point to the first and second centuries BC was the reference in many psalms to Yahweh's 'anointed', whom Duhm regarded in several instances as one of the Maccabean princes, and, in certain cases, even as a reference to a foreign, but friendly, ruler.

The case for this late dating of much of the Psalter rested on arguments of a very general nature, and it did not pass unchallenged. In this connection we should certainly note the very different assessment in the commentary by A. F. Kirkpatrick which has remained a classic among psalm studies.[6] Kirkpatrick urged that the case for such a late date could not be regarded as proven, and countered it with arguments of his own which led him to claim a much earlier, pre-exilic, origin for many psalms. He did not rule out entirely the possibility that some psalms were composed by David, but in any case he urged that the most natural interpretation of those psalms which referred to Yahweh's anointed was one which regarded them as composed for reigning kings of Judah during the period of the monarchy. Furthermore he urged that the psalms which expressly celebrate Yahweh's power from Zion (Psalms 46, 48, 76) could best be regarded as having been written soon after the deliverance of Jerusalem from the Assyrians under Sennacherib in 701 BC. Overall therefore the case for regarding the Psalter as essentially an expression of the piety and religious conflicts of the Maccabean age was far from being universally accepted. Further dissent from such a view along comparable lines to those argued by Kirkpatrick was made by S. R. Driver in his much used *Introduction to the Literature of the Old Testament*.[7]

A basic aspect of this late dating of the Psalter was the particular interpretation which it presupposed of the numerous references to oppression, injustice and suffering inflicted on righteous Israelites who voiced their protests and pleas to God in the psalms. These references were of several kinds and included allusions to false accusations, ridicule, persecution even to the point of death, and to other broader descriptions of misfortune. The psalmists refer to themselves as poor and afflicted so that the picture which arises in many cases is that of strife within a community in which the loyal Israelite felt himself to be the victim of unscrupulous and godless oppressors. A. Rahlfs advocated an interpretation of this which saw the poor and afflicted speaker in the Psalms as loyal, but downtrodden Jews of the post-exilic age who were caught up in what was basically a very sharp form of class warfare.[8] This thesis was widely followed so that the psalms were taken to reveal many of the inner tensions and conflicts which characterized the otherwise little known circumstances of Jewish religious and social life in the immediate pre-Christian centuries.

Such a view, however, was opposed by a contrasting hypothesis advocated in a most thoroughgoing way by R. Smend, in an essay published in 1888,[9] that the 'I' who speaks in the Psalms is not an individual Israelite, but a personification of the community as a whole. The enemies complained about therefore are not private enemies, but those of the nation in general, and the conflicts are international in character. Such a view undoubtedly undermined one of the most insistent arguments used in favour of a Maccabean date: that the type of individual piety reflected in the psalms, and the conflicts it encountered, only emerged at a late period of the religious development of the Old Testament. All of these broad questions, about the identity of Yahweh's anointed referred to in the psalms, the nature of the conflicts reflected in the psalmists' pleas to God for deliverance, and the significance of the use of the first person singular in a large number of psalms, have remained continuing problems of the interpretation of the Psalter. Further study has raised new questions and suggested new solutions, but alongside these achievements it has also served to demonstrate the serious limitations of method which characterized the early conclusions of literary criticism. New ideas and insights were called for, if there was to be a new assessment of the Psalms in the light of the new historical perspective gained from the literary criticism of the Pentateuch and the prophets.

The name that stands out above all others as that of the pioneer of a new approach to the Psalms is Hermann Gunkel's. Already we have noted the originality of his insights and the freshness of his method in the study of the book of Genesis, centering on his concern to define the type, or *Gattung*, of the literary units which the Old Testament writings contain. In a series of writings and essays, beginning in 1904 and continuing to the end of his life, Gunkel applied this method to the study of the psalms with great success. The first of Gunkel's publications in this field was a commentary on selected psalms, first published in 1904, which ran into several editions.[10] Brief expositions of a number of psalms by Gunkel were translated into English and published in America, although their impact on the world of English-speaking scholars does not at first appear to have been very extensive. The main outline of the method of *Gattungsgeschichte*, as it applied to the Psalms, was presented by Gunkel in an article in the first edition of the major dictionary *Die Religion in Geschichte und Gegenwart*.[11] This was revised by Gunkel for the second edition, and an English translation of it appeared as recently as 1967.[12] A major commentary on the entire Psalter, as distinct from the selected psalms of 1904, was published in 1926[13] and an extensive volume of introduction to this was not fully complete by the time of Gunkel's death in 1932. It was completed and prepared for publication by Gunkel's friend and pupil J. Begrich in 1933.[14]

It is of interest that the first major attempt to develop in a commentary on the whole Psalter the method of *Gattungsgeschichte*, which Gunkel had inaugurated, was made by W. Staerk in the composite volume *Die Schriften des Alten Testaments*.[15] However Staerk's analysis of the types of psalm, or lyrics as he preferred to call them, divided them into such a large variety of classes as to render the whole enterprise rather self-defeating, for a primary part of its value was in showing how much the psalms shared in common. Because of this excess of classes the common features, and with this the recognition of a common tradition of psalm writing together with a similarity of setting for many psalms, were obscured. It was left therefore for Gunkel himself to explore the full possibilities of his method in a commentary on the whole Psalter.

Basically Gunkel was concerned to note four or five main types of psalm, and to add to these a number of lesser sub-types. Further to these were some psalms of mixed type which could be regarded as deriving from a late period when the original pure types had become separated from the settings in which they originated, and which served to preserve their form. Gunkel's main psalm types were (i) the hymn, from which he sometimes distinguished communal songs of thanksgiving, (ii) the community laments, (iii) the individual laments, (iv) the individual songs of thanksgiving, and (v) the royal psalms.

It can be seen immediately here that the distinctions between these types are based upon criteria of more than one kind. The broadest basis of division is between songs of thanksgiving (hymns) and laments, with a further distinction between those which are voiced by the community and those which are voiced by an individual. The royal psalms form a yet different category, several examples of which are of the hymn type. Similarly two of Gunkel's lesser types, the songs of Zion and the songs of Yahweh's enthronement are essentially hymns, but are set apart by distinctive features of content.

So far as the main lines of Gunkel's interpretation of the Psalter are concerned we can note a number of points which stand out very prominently. Of prime importance was Gunkel's insistence that the laments and songs of thanksgiving couched in the first person singular 'I' form were intended to be used by individual Israelites, and had for the most part been composed privately by pious Israelites. Although he regarded the type as having originated in the cult, he concluded that most of the extant examples were separated from this cultic setting and were expressive of a more personal and private piety than the original setting afforded. In line with this Gunkel regarded the psalms voiced by individuals as later classes than those in which the community voiced its praise or lament to God, since he accepted that it was only after the exile that a more private type of piety emerged in Israel.[16] A very thorough and detailed investigation of the whole question of the nature of the 'I' who speaks in many psalms was undertaken at Gunkel's suggestion by his pupil E. Balla.[17] The results were published in 1913, and represented a very sound refutation of the earlier thesis, advocated by many scholars but most rigorously by R. Smend, that this first person form was simply a personification of the pious community.

As a further working out of the setting of the laments of the individual, which are much more numerous in the Psalter than individual songs of thanksgiving, Gunkel claimed that in a great many instances the primary misfortune which had occasioned the lament was illness. Hence the descriptions of physical distress were regarded as references to such illness, and the link between this distress and the assaults and gibes of enemies, which were often mentioned along with it, was found by Gunkel in the attitude of self-righteous neighbours. They would have looked upon illness as a mark of divine disfavour, and accordingly have turned against anyone stricken by it.

Of the royal psalms, which were grouped together by Gunkel to form an important separate category, it was claimed that they must refer to a native Israelite monarch of the pre-exilic period. On this point therefore he was in agreement with the views of A. F. Kirkpatrick. Gunkel listed among such royal psalms, hymns for a coronation (Psalms 2; 110), a hymn for a royal wedding (Psalm 45) and a hymn on the anniversary of the founding of the dynasty (Psalm 132). The extravagant language to be found in several of these psalms, which assured the king of victory in battle, wide dominion, divine wisdom and peace, Gunkel ascribed to the natural tendency to hyperbole in the ancient oriental court style.

One further aspect of the interpretation of the psalms received a considerable amount of attention from Gunkel. This was the question of the relationship of the Psalms to the prophets. That a number of passages in the prophetic books revealed close similarities in form, language and ideas to passages in the psalms could not be denied. The question was to define the nature and scope of this similarity and from this to arrive at some explanation of how it had come about. In general Gunkel argued that the priority lay with the prophets who had experienced a more intensely personal form of religion than their contemporaries, and who had developed ideas and attitudes, especially with respect to the cult, as a reflection of this. However the connection between psalmody and prophecy was not all from one direction and Gunkel saw a most significant feature of Israelite religious development to have lain in their mutual inter-relationship.

The greatness of Gunkel's achievement in pioneering a new approach to the Psalms and thereby opening up new possibilities of understanding them in relation to Israel's worship and spirituality remains unchallenged. A whole new era of psalm studies became possible on the basis of the classification of psalm types, and the related lines of interpretation which he established. Not only so but he had also shown up very clearly the unsatisfactoriness of a number of false trails which had for long been followed by psalm commentators.

Because of the period of almost thirty years during which Gunkel's varied contributions to psalm studies appeared, it is important to note the development within them and also the way in which they were influenced by the work of more than one of his pupils. Foremost among these we must certainly place the Norwegian scholar Sigmund Mowinckel, who had fallen under the spell of Gunkel's brilliance and originality as a student at Giessen in 1908, and who thereafter retained the warmest affection and gratitude for his teacher. Even before Gunkel's commentary on the whole Psalter had been published in 1926,

Mowinckel had moved a very long way in surprisingly new directions so that the freshness of his own insights above those of Gunkel must in no way be minimized. Nevertheless it is evident that Mowinckel's work builds throughout on the foundations laid by Gunkel, even where it moved a great distance from these earlier footings, and Mowinckel himself remained consistently conscious of his debt to Gunkel.

From the outset, in considering Mowinckel's achievements it is important to recognize that another influence besides that of the German scholar had made a profound impact upon him, and had in its own way led the Norwegian scholar to disagree with several prominent aspects of Gunkel's interpretations of the Psalms. This derived from the Danish anthropologist Vilhelm Grønbech, under whom Mowinckel also studied, and whose special interest lay in the field of early Indo-European culture. His major work, *The Culture of the Teutons*, was published in an English translation in 1931,[18] and shows clearly many of the insights about the structure and behaviour of primitive societies which so deeply influenced Mowinckel. Foremost among these must be set a radically new appraisal of the role of cult in such societies. Instead of regarding it as a relatively static and formal collection of rites, linked together more or less haphazardly, Grønbech argued that the cultus in such societies was dynamic, and essentially dramatic in its character. It embraced the whole life of society in its powerful grip, moulding ideas, intruding values and acting as a cement to bind the community together. Such a picture of primitive cultus was at once more extensive, more deeply personal in its impact and more enduring in its legacy than anthropologists, and especially those anthropologists who had concerned themselves with the structure of early Semitic societies, had hitherto been inclined to accept.

The first of Mowinckel's studies to deal with questions of psalm interpretation was published in Norwegian in 1916, and dealt with the royal psalms.[19] Significantly it is dedicated jointly to H. Gunkel and V. Grønbech, and its indebtedness to both scholars is apparent throughout. Starting from the basis of those psalms which Gunkel had already noted as royal, Mowinckel argued that the extravagant language and high status accorded to the king was not a result of the flattering and exaggerated language of the court, but a witness to the mythological and cultic role which he was believed to play. Mowinckel could claim that the king was 'a veritable incarnation of the national god', who performed a vital sacral role within the cult. On the basis of this claim to a distinctive cultic role performed by the king, Mowinckel could then go on to note features which the admittedly royal psalms had in common with others, so that he was thereby drawn on to include several of the other psalms into the category of royal.

The first impact of the young Mowinckel's work on the Psalter was not apparently very marked, no doubt partly as a result of the time of its publication and its appearance in Norwegian. During the years 1921–24, however, Mowinckel published *Psalmenstudien I–VI*,[20] which were in the long run destined to bring about changes in the understanding of the Psalter, fully as great as those which Gunkel had already initiated. At innumerable points it is clear that Mowinckel was building upon the foundations laid by Gunkel, and that a great many of the questions which he raised had been initially suggested by Gunkel's work. Yet the conclusions which the Norwegian scholar put forward were in many cases very different from those of the German.

Throughout the six separate studies one basic tendency is very marked, and this is to relate the extant Psalter, not in its entirety but in the majority of its individual psalm compositions comprising laments, hymns and liturgies, much more directly to the cult than Gunkel had done. In a large number of cases, especially in the laments of the individual, Gunkel had argued that the psalm which we have was a private composition made for devotional purposes, of a type which had originally belonged to the cult. Mowinckel, however, argued that with only few exceptions the psalms which have been preserved in the Psalter were originally composed for use in the cult. In line with this view the question of the relationship between the psalms and prophecy, which Gunkel had regarded as an important factor in explaining the development of this form of private psalm-writing, was taken up by Mowinckel and answered by positing a development in the opposite direction. Where Gunkel had primarily seen the prophets as the initiators, and the psalm-writers as dependent on them, Mowinckel argued that the main line of influence was in the other direction. The psalms indicate the ideas, language and religious forms which were current in the early cultus of Israel, and it is the prophets who have adapted them and applied them to new situations.

It is not possible to summarize in brief compass all the main points of Mowinckel's interpretations of the psalms, and to follow this through by examining the way in which Gunkel, and other scholars, responded to them, leaving Mowinckel himself in turn to reconsider, and in some cases to modify, his views. Since few aspects of the subject were left unaffected by the work of these two scholars we can, however, look at some of the main questions raised by Mowinckel's work and note the ways in which they have provided a starting point for others to follow up and develop.

Gunkel had noted as one of the smaller categories of psalms, a group of hymns which celebrated the enthronement of Yahweh as universal King. These were Psalms 47, 93, 95–99, which show a clear relationship in their language and ideas to parts of Isaiah 40–55. Gunkel accordingly regarded these psalms as eschatological in their reference, and as dependent for their ideas and language upon the preaching of the exilic prophet. In his *Psalmenstudien II*, however, Mowinckel argued that not only these particular psalms, but a great many others also, had originally been composed for use in the New Year festival of early Israel, celebrated in the autumn, which glorified Yahweh as King and affirmed his re-exaltation to the throne of the universe. It was the prophet Deutero-Isaiah who had borrowed the language of these hymns to apply their ideas to the event of the return of the Babylonian exiles to their homeland.

Mowinckel here was not mooting the existence of a hitherto completely unknown and unrecorded festival, for there had undoubtedly been a festival celebrated in early Israel in the autumn when the new year began. Even the earliest lists of festivals contained in the Old Testament refer to a celebration at this time of the year (Exodus 23: 16; 34: 22), and the later, post-exilic, record in Leviticus 23: 23ff. points to a Day of Atonement, a celebration involving the blowing of rams' horns and a Festival of Tabernacles as taking place in the autumn. What Mowinckel was claiming was that these celebrations had originally been part of one great festival for which the psalms of Yahweh's Enthronement had been composed. Such a festival bore many points of similarity to the Babylonian *Akitu* festival. Apart from the evidence of these psalms, and some references in other parts of the Old Testament, Mowinckel adduced support for his hypothesis from the liturgies of the Babylonian celebration, and to a large extent also, from comments and references in later Jewish writers of the Rabbinic age. These revealed a substantial element of creation symbolism attaching to the Feast of Tabernacles.

The psalms composed for the Enthronement Festival asserted Yahweh's kingship, which Mowinckel interpreted as a kingship over the whole created cosmos, comprising control of the forces of nature, the regulation of the seasons, the giving of fertility in fields and herds and the stability and order of human society. The references to this divine rule were not originally eschatological, but part of the whole cultic ideology and mythology by which the relationship of the divine and human worlds was understood. Nevertheless in his original study Mowinckel argued that there was a connection between the ideas current in this festival and the origin of eschatology in Israel. Increasingly the political misfortunes which befell Israel and Judah during the period of the monarchy brought an element of tension between the historical reality and the cultic-mythological assertion, so that eventually the whole idea of Yahweh's divine rule was projected into the future to form an eschatological hope of the coming greatness and prosperity of his people.

No part of Mowinckel's interpretation of the Psalter has been more sharply criticized and contested than this, and scholarly reaction has varied between outright rejection, modest acceptance and the presentation of various alternative hypotheses regarding the character of the Autumn Festival. In some of these the Hymns of Yahweh's Enthronement play a part, and in others they do not. It is surprising, in view of Mowinckel's earlier study of kingship, that the role ascribed to the king in this festival is not all that extensive, although clearly regarded by Mowinckel as very important. The representation of Yahweh's presence was seen to be provided by the ark. In 1927 Hans Schmidt argued briefly for a more prominent role to be ascribed to the king in this festival so that the earthly (Israelite) king was seen as the embodiment of Yahweh, the divine King.[21] Such a contention is of significance in connection with a whole range of fresh attempts at rediscovering the status and role of the king in early Israel. Mowinckel himself later revised his understanding of the festival, and in doing so considerably enlarged upon his view of the part played by the king in it, thereby associating it more closely with the royal psalms.[22]

From another side A. Weiser sought to develop Gunkel's method of interpreting the Psalms,[23] but with a very different understanding of the nature of early Israelite cultus from that being advocated by Mowinckel. He argued that most of our Psalter was composed for use in the cult, and in particular he argued that the Autumn Festival had possessed the character of a Festival of Covenant Renewal. Thus a very large number of psalms had been composed for use at this celebration, including many which Mowinckel had ascribed to the Enthronement Festival. However these did not include the Hymns of Yahweh's Enthronement, which Weiser regarded as eschatological in the manner of Gunkel. The Covenant Festival was essentially an act of national renewal, recalling the founding of Israel at the covenant of Sinai.

Yet another view of the Autumn Festival was advocated by H. J. Kraus,[24] who associated it primarily with the Hymns of Zion and certain of the royal psalms. He regarded it as a Royal Zion Festival, celebrating the founding of the Davidic dynasty and the divine choice of Mount Zion as the abode of the ark and the site of the temple. Like Weiser he regarded the Hymns of Yahweh's Enthronement as eschatological in character and dependent on the preaching of Deutero-Isaiah. Other scholars, however, have advocated views much closer to those of Mowinckel,[25] seeing the essential rightness of his understanding of cultus, and the creative role that this played in determining the language and ideas of the psalms, but wishing nonetheless to recognize the distinctively Israelite forms of cultic life in Israel. As a result they have laid less emphasis upon the similarities with the Babylonian celebration, and in doing so have found support from Mowinckel's own later reconsideration of his presentation.

H. Gunkel's classification of a special category of royal psalms led to a considerable re-appraisal of the role of the king in ancient Israel. His elevation of these psalms from constituting a minor group, which is how they appeared in his early classification, to form a major one, reflects a growing sense of their importance. Whereas the king is scarcely mentioned in the law codes of the Old Testament, and the historical books contain many very critical accounts of the monarchy as an institution, the royal psalms very consistently describe his office and status in strikingly exalted religious language. He is Yahweh's 'son' (Psalm 2: 7) the 'fairest of the sons of men' (Psalm 45: 2), and in one controversial passage he appears even to be addressed as 'god' (Psalm 45: 6). Gunkel himself was inclined to play down the significance of this language by regarding it as a reflection of an exaggerated and flattering court-style. Already in 1916, however, Mowinckel had seen the relationship which such language bore to the mythological images and ideas of ancient cultus, and had accordingly endeavoured to reconstruct the cultic role which the Israelite king must have once played.

From another direction also, interest in the religious significance of kingship in ancient Israel fostered a fresh examination of these royal psalms. The anthropological and folklorist researches of J. G. Frazer had made much of the role which kingship played in primitive societies as a manifestation of the divine. S. H. Hooke set out very consciously to relate these approaches to the study of the Bible and encouraged a number of scholars to bring together their conclusions regarding the nature and significance of primitive cult and ritual, especially in relation to the Bible. These appeared initially in two volumes, the first entitled *Myth and Ritual* [26] and the second *The Labyrinth*. [27] In the second of these A. R. Johnson expressed a number of far-reaching conclusions regarding the part played by ancient kingship in relation to the cult, which further developed some of the suggestions of Mowinckel. [28] In particular Johnson argued that the Davidic kingship of Jerusalem drew upon an older tradition of Canaanite kingship in the city, and that this provided a vital connecting link between the old ancient Near Eastern pattern of kingship and that which emerged in Israel. Such a view was still further taken up later by H. J. Kraus in seeking an explanation of a number of cultic features and semi-mythological themes present in the Psalter, not all of which were directly concerned with kingship. [29] A number of Scandinavian scholars also entered extensively into the debate about the Israelite form of monarchy, and sought to find in its ancient Near Eastern roots an explanation for its vitality and eventual resurgence in the guise of a messianic expectation. Notable among these were I. Engnell, [30] G. Widengren [31] and A. Bentzen. [32]

In 1948 a sharp attack upon such views, and with them the whole idea of a common culture pattern extending across the ancient Near East, was presented by H. Frankfort in a volume entitled *Kingship and the Gods*. [33] Fundamental to Frankfort's objections was an awareness, based upon detailed study of literary materials relating to Mesopotamian and Egyptian kingship, of the indigenous character and distinctiveness of the political and religious developments in the separate political and cultural regions of the ancient orient. In a number of respects Frankfort overreacted against the somewhat speculative arguments of S. H. Hooke and the other advocates of a very exalted king ideology having been current in Israel. In particular Frankfort challenged the tendency to argue for this on the grounds of evidence from outside the Old Testament. In this respect it is noteworthy that he did not attempt any separate appraisal of the very rich language used about kingship in the Psalms.

So far as Old Testament studies were concerned this was very central to the whole discussion, and the issue was not whether such rich language existed, which it plainly did, but what it had once meant. Here many difficulties beset the biblical scholar, since a wide range of possibilities exist for an adequate appreciation of what was meant by such a phrase as 'son of God'. How far traditions of cultic mythology, social convention or simply court flattery have influenced the use of such a term cannot easily be defined. In this regard very positive contributions towards elucidating the status of the king have been made by S. Mowinckel[34] and A. R. Johnson,[35] both of whom have sought to clarify the social function of the king and his role in the cultus as a means towards obtaining a better understanding of what such royal titles indicate. Certainly what we find preserved in the royal psalms are expressions of a very positive and favourable attitude to the monarchy from a circle of the Jerusalem cult which stood very close to the Davidic kingship. A further result of such studies into the meaning of kingship as expressed in the Psalms has been a better understanding of the nature and significance of a number of passages in the prophetic books which refer to a future king, and which have loosely been regarded as messianic. In the light of this better understanding it can no longer be taken for granted that these prophecies about the kingship were not original to the prophets to which they are now ascribed, and certainly the significance of their language can be set within a very different context from that which later Jewish and Christian messianic speculation ascribed to them.

A prominent feature of some of the more radical attempts to interpret the role of the king in Israel's cult on the basis of evidence provided by the Psalter has been a tendency to draw more and more psalms into the category of royal. The belief that the king had played an indispensable role in the Autumn Festival came to carry with it the belief that not only the Hymns of Yahweh's Enthronement, but probably also many other psalms, such as the Hymns of Zion, were to be linked with this festival, and thereby with the king who figured in it. The Swedish scholar I. Engnell, in fact, came to argue that the majority of psalms in the Psalter had originally been composed for use by the king,[36] and only later were they modified for lay use. From another direction, and prompted by the difficulties of interpreting a feature which appears prominently in a great many psalms, the view was canvassed that the king was at first intended to be the speaker in a large number of them. This feature was the problem of identifying the nature of the misfortunes of which the psalm speakers complain, and the identity of the enemies, from whose clutches and plotting the psalmists frequently appeal to God for help. Their attacks, threats and malicious accusations provide the psalmists with a deep sense of unjust suffering and a real occasion of fear.

Who were these enemies who so savagely threatened the pious man's life? By dating almost all the psalms in the Maccabean age B. Duhm had been able to explain them as the opponents of devout Jews in the time of sectarian strife in the second and first centuries BC. Reflected in these psalms was the inter-party warfare in which the Pharisees in particular had suffered at the hands of despotic rulers. In a not dissimilar vein A. Rahlfs had argued that the way in which the psalmists describe themselves as 'poor' and 'humble' revealed the identity of the oppressed, and pointed to the oppressors as the wealthy, landowning, ruling class. These latter abused their power by taking advantage of the under-privileged, but pious, citizens of Judah after the exile. The mention of such enemies therefore indicated a kind of class struggle, breaking out at times into open conflict, in which the poor and wealthy were involved.

The problem of identifying these enemies was brought more fully into the foreground of investigation by Gunkel's claim, first presented in detail by his pupil E. Balla, that the 'I' who speaks in many of the laments was an individual lay Israelite, and that the first person usage was not a literary personification of Israel, nor a community of the pious within it. Furthermore Gunkel's freeing of these psalms from the restrictive insistence on their origin in the second and first centuries BC gave a much wider range of possibilities for understanding their references to conflict and to the activities of enemies. Gunkel himself argued that most of the individual laments were written out of a situation of distress occasioned by illness. Hence, as we have already noted, he regarded the enemies as self-righteous neighbours of the afflicted person.

In the first of his *Psalmenstudien* Mowinckel took up this question of the relationship between the psalmists' misfortune, which in the majority of cases he followed Gunkel in regarding as illness, and the enemies who are referred to. The answer presented by Mowinckel was that the enemies were believed to be responsible in some way for causing the worshipper's misfortune, and must have been thought to have cast a spell on him. Hence the intellectual world of many psalms was that of magic, and the loosely defined area where magic, cultus and fear combined together in a semi-religious view of the world. Mowinckel went on to argue that the very expression 'workers of iniquity', by which the psalmists' enemies were sometimes described, essentially referred to 'manipulators of magic power'.

From a different direction the German scholar H. Schmidt sought to shed light on the problem of identifying the enemies by noting that frequently the psalmists complained of the injustice of their accusations and besought God for some tangible act, or sign, of vindication. In consequence he postulated that these psalms were uttered by men who had been falsely accused of some crime or offence, and who besought God to demonstrate their innocence and to secure their acquittal. This led Schmidt to think of some kind of religious trial, conducted before priests, in which the worshipper was examined under oath and acquitted if shown to be innocent.[37] Such a view has been developed more extensively by W. Beyerlin.[38]

Working with some of the same assumptions about the nature of the psalmists' distress, but reconstructing a very different situation to account for the writing of the psalms concerned, L. Delekat[39] has suggested that these latter were pleas for admission to a sanctuary as a place of divinely protected asylum. The enemies were thus the accusers and pursuers of the psalmist, and the latter wrote out his defence plea in the form of a psalm. He was then either granted, or refused, asylum on the basis of it. Delekat also argued that there may also have been a priestly oracle which constituted the divine 'answer' to it. Certainly all of these views have contributed towards the illumination of the types of distress of which the psalmists complain; unjust accusations, illness, boorish neighbours and wealthy oppressors would all appear to fit some of the descriptions of the troubles complained of. Yet the attempts to tie down these descriptions to very specific cultic situations have been of only limited success in explaining the setting of the psalms concerned since many of the features they contain do not readily fit into such schemes.

The problem was looked at in a different way by H. Birkeland,[40] a pupil of Mowinckel's. Birkeland noted that in some cases there are references to enemies in the community laments where it is most appropriate that we should think of national enemies. Similar references to enemies are found in certain of the royal psalms, where again it is most natural that we should think of national, rather than personal, enemies of the king. When we turn to the descriptions of the enemies in the individual laments we find that they are very similar in their character and content to those given in the other two cases. The conclusion which Birkeland drew was that the enemies must be essentially of the same kind in all three cases. Thus the speaker in the individual laments must either be the king, or some other national leader such as the leader of the armed forces. Throughout the Psalter the enemies must generally be regarded as national enemies. Mowinckel himself later expressed some measure of support for such a view, but not in such a wide-ranging fashion as to bring most of the laments under the same heading.[41] Certainly the problem overall has not easily submitted to any one solution and we can recognize the partial truths of several of these views. Even the notion of some half-magical conception of the world is certainly not to be ruled out, since there are clear traces of this in the Old Testament. Yet no one hypothesis about the identity of the enemies has been able to account for all the features included in the descriptions of them, and we must conclude that the intentions of the psalm-writers were not always the same. We cannot therefore arrive at a solution to the problem by looking for any one single setting for the personal lament psalms.

We have noted already that at a very early period in his studies of the Old Testament H. Gunkel published an essay on Nahum 1 in which he argued that this chapter of a prophetic book was set out in the form of an acrostic liturgical psalm.[42] This pointed to a connection between prophecy and psalmody of a rather different kind from that expressed in the view of Duhm that psalmody was a late flowering of the piety and morality originated by the prophets. Although Gunkel had in no way wished to set aside this picture of a general dependence of psalmody upon prophecy, he had in this instance set out a case for believing that parts of the prophetic literature may have been influenced by psalm liturgies. In later essays Gunkel made use of a similar kind of argument to show the presence of such liturgical forms in the conclusion of the book of Micah and also in Isaiah 33.[43] These essays were concerned to show how the forms of Israel's worship, which are directly reflected in the form of a number of psalms, are also to be found reflected, or imitated, in prophecy. In his studies of the Psalms, especially in an extensive section in the *Einleitung*,[44] Gunkel argued that the main direction of influence had been from prophecy to the psalms. As a result a great many ideas, themes and verbal images which originated in prophecy found their way into the Psalter. Primarily here Gunkel pointed to Israel's eschatological hope, which he believed originated with the prophets and yet is to be found in a number of psalms, supremely the Hymns of Yahweh's Enthronement. These hymns, Gunkel argued, were modelled upon the prophecies of Deutero-Isaiah, taking up and elaborating particular ideas and images used by this prophet. Even more widely Gunkel found a development of this eschatological hope of a universal reign of Yahweh expressed in certain of the royal psalms, such as Psalms 2 and 110, and in the Hymns of Zion (Psalms 46, 48).

Besides this eschatological hope Gunkel pointed to a number of other themes and ideas of the prophets' preaching which had been carried over into the psalms. Prominent among these, Gunkel believed, were certain criticisms of the cult, especially of the institution of sacrifice, which he regarded as dependent upon the attacks on the practice of the cult made by the great prophets. Other features too, including a general concern with the obligations of social justice were held to reflect the way in which prophecy had left its mark upon psalmody. It was not only in the world of ideas, however, that the relationship between the psalmists and the prophets showed itself, but also in the area of literary forms, which Gunkel did so much to clarify. In a number of psalms a very striking oracular form was employed, as for example in Psalm 2: 7–9, where a divine assurance to the king promised him a divinely effected victory over his enemies and their complete humiliation. Here Gunkel argued that the oracular form, found in prophecy, had been adapted and used in the psalm. As we have already noted, however, Gunkel also fully accepted that the influence of forms and ideas could be traced in the other direction, where prophecy made use of liturgical forms from the cult. Because of this the forms of liturgies, hymns and laments, which are primarily found in the Psalter, could all be traced in prophetic passages. There was, therefore, according to Gunkel, a very important interaction between psalmody and prophecy in which forms and ideas proper to each had exerted an influence upon the other. Chiefly, however, it is evident that Gunkel saw the main strength of such influence to have been from prophecy to the psalms. This conclusion was entirely in line with Gunkel's overall conviction regarding the creative originality of the prophets.

When we consider the ways in which Mowinckel modified and developed Gunkel's psalm interpretations in his own *Psalmenstudien I–VI*, it is immediately apparent that the question of the mutual influence exerted between prophets and psalmists had taken on a very deep significance. On a number of very important points Mowinckel took up questions raised by Gunkel, but came to different conclusions in regard to them. Thus Mowinckel's quite new understanding of the relationship between the preaching of Deutero-Isaiah and the Hymns of Yahweh's Enthronement fits into this category. By setting aside Gunkel's explanation that the hymns had been modelled on the prophecies, Mowinckel found himself free to look for a quite different original setting for the former in the cult, where they were no longer to be regarded as eschatological hymns but as revealing testimony to the ideas and intentions of the cult. Similarly in the case of the Zion hymns, which A. F. Kirkpatrick had regarded as composed to celebrate the lifting of the siege of Jerusalem in 701 BC after the Assyrian attack under Sennacherib, Mowinckel now argued that this was not so. Rather the old cult hymns which celebrated in the timeless language of myth the victory of Yahweh from Mount Zion had so coloured the accounts of what had happened in 701 BC that the significant, but politically and militarily intelligible, act of Assyrian leniency towards Jerusalem in that year had acquired the aura and fame of a miraculous divine victory.[45] So extensive and radical was Mowinckel's re-appraisal of the role of the cult in early Israel that he could quite freely argue that time and again it was from this source that ideas, verbal images and literary forms had been taken up by prophecy. As a general working rule Mowinckel could later write, 'The religion of the psalms is the spiritual background of the prophets'.[46]

From this standpoint of a broad recognition of cases where the ideas and forms of the cult, which are attested in the Psalter, have influenced the pronouncements of the prophets, Mowinckel went on to consider the whole question of the relationship between prophecy and psalmody in Israel.[47] There are a large number of cases where an oracular form, such as we find frequently in the prophets, also makes its appearance in a psalm. Gunkel had explained this phenomenon as an illustration of the way in which the psalmists borrow from, and imitate, the prophets. Mowinckel however, argued for a more direct explanation of the origin of the oracular element in the psalms in question. There were present in Israel's cult, he maintained, cultic prophets who must be looked to as the speakers of the oracular sayings which are contained in certain psalms. What Mowinckel was proposing was a much wider understanding of the nature of prophecy in Israel, with a recognition that certain of the professional personnel of the sanctuaries should be recognized as prophets. The distinction between priests and prophets, which had come to be regarded as a very sharp one in critical reconstructions of the development of Israel's religion, was neither clearly nor rigidly adhered to. On this score Gunkel criticized Mowinckel's view as entailing so much broader a conception of priesthood than was usually accepted, and so wide a definition of prophecy, as to blur the lines of distinction between priest and prophet.[48] Yet, while the element of the blurring of definitions must be admitted, Mowinckel was undoubtedly right in recognizing the close ties which had once bound prophecy to the cult and its concerns. We have already noted the effect that this recognition had upon the understanding of prophecy and the formation of the prophetic books. The fuller implications of Mowinckel's thesis regarding cultic prophecy for the study of the Psalter have received only limited attention in subsequent studies of the Psalms, and their main impact has been upon the study of the prophets.

However in relation to the study of one prophet in particular the dramatic reversal of priorities which Mowinckel proposed regarding psalmody and prophecy has been especially fruitful. This is Deutero-Isaiah, where in a striking way Gunkel's friend and pupil J. Begrich was able to develop and establish the claim that several of the speech forms found in Deutero-Isaiah, with their strong poetic imagery, derive from psalmody.[49] He was able to trace here the prophet's use of the form and language of the oracle of assurance, which Gunkel had seen to belong to the cultic situation in which a priest gave answer to the worshipper's lament.[50] In a host of other ways also Begrich was able to demonstrate that the prophecy of Deutero-Isaiah is steeped in the language, ideas, idioms and poetic forms of Israelite psalmody. Begrich's early death at the end of the second world war undoubtedly lost to Old Testament scholarship a most accomplished exponent of the method of *Gattungsgeschichte*. Overall it can be seen that Mowinckel's willingness to reconsider the issue of priority in the interconnections of prophecy and psalmody established a basis for a radical reassessment of both. As a result the sharpness of the cleavage between the prophets and the cult, which had formed a significant aspect of the history of Israel's religious development in the reconstructions of Wellhausen and Duhm, was demonstrably shown to be false.

In looking back over the impact of psalm studies upon Old Testament interpretation over the past century it is noticeable how it has moved from a minor to a major role. In the work of Wellhausen and his immediate followers the Psalms, for all the admiration accorded to their literary qualities and spirituality, were relegated to a very subordinate and secondary position in the growth of the Old Testament. They were looked upon simply as reflecting the undercurrent of personal piety and hope which flourished when the main creative impulses of Israel's religion had ebbed away. As a result of the work of Gunkel and Mowinckel, however, the Psalms were elevated to a new position of priority as a witness to the groundwork of cult and piety which underlie the formation of the historical books as well as the phenomenon of prophecy in Israel. They illustrate the language and aspirations which belonged essentially to the cult, and which lie behind the activities of prophets, wise men and historians. They can therefore be seen to stand in a remarkably central position in the Old Testament, and to provide an essential backcloth against which other religious developments can be viewed.

1. A brief list of scholars who had advocated such a late date is given by J. Wellhausen in F. Bleek, *Einleitung in das Alte Testament*, fourth edition by J. Wellhausen, Berlin, 1878, note 1, p. 504.
2. J. Olshausen, *Die Psalmen* (Kurzgefasstes exegetisches Handbuch zum Alten Testament), Leipzig, 1853. A memorial address to Olshausen is given by the German orientalist E. Schrader, 'Gedächtnis Rede auf Justus Olshausen' in *Abhandlungen der königlichen Akademie der Wissenschaften zu Berlin* (1883), Berlin, 1884, pp. 1–21.
3. The entry in Bleek's *Einleitung* is generally critical of so late a date for the Psalms, and Wellhausen does not appear to have wished to disagree markedly with this.
4. J. Wellhausen, *The Book of Psalms* (Sacred Books of the Old Testament 14), Leipzig, Baltimore, London, 1895.
5. B. Duhm, *Die Psalmen (KHAT* XIV), Freiburg, 1899, second edition 1922.
6. A. F. Kirkpatrick, *The Psalms* (Cambridge Bible), Cambridge, 1902.
7. S. R. Driver, *Introduction to the Literature of the Old Testament*, ninth edition 1913, p. 382.
8. A. Rahlfs, *'Ani and 'Anaw in den Psalmen*, I, Göttingen, 1892.
9. R. Smend, 'Über das Ich der Psalmen', in *ZAW* 8 (1888), pp. 49–147.
10. H. Gunkel, *Ausgewählte Psalmen*, Göttingen, 1904.
11. H. Gunkel, art. 'Psalmen' in *Die Religion in Geschichte und Gegenwart*, Bd. IV, 1913, cols. 1927–1949; revised for the second edition in 1927.
12. *The Psalms*, Facet Books Biblical Series 19, Philadelphia, 1967.
13. H. Gunkel, *Die Psalmen (HKAT* XIV), Göttingen, 1929, fifth edition 1968.
14. H. Gunkel, *Einleitung in die Psalmen*, Göttingen, 1933.
15. W. Staerk, *Lyrik, Psalmen, Hoheslied und Verwandtes* (SAT III/1), second edition 1920.
16. The great importance which Gunkel attached to this distinction and its significance for the chronology of Israel's religious development is to be seen in his article 'Individualismus und Sozialismus im Alten Testament' *Die Religion in Geschichte und Gegenwart*, Bd. III, cols. 493–501 (first edition 1912).
17. E. Balla, *Das Ich der Psalmen (FRLANT* 16), Göttingen, 1912.
18. V. Grønbech, *The Culture of the Teutons*, Oxford, 1931.
19. S. Mowinckel, *Kongesalmerne i det Gamle Testaments*, Oslo, 1916.
20. Reprinted Amsterdam, 1961.
21. H. Schmidt, *Die Thronfahrt Jahwes am Feste der Jahreswende im alten Israel* (Sammlung gemeinverstandlicher Vortrage und Schriften 122), Tübingen, 1927.
22. So *The Psalms in Israel's Worship*, Oxford, 1962, Vol. I, pp. 106–192. In the foreword to the reprint of his *Psalmenstudien* II in 1961 Mowinckel tells how he had, at Gunkel's request, written an entry for the second edition of *Die Religion in Geschichte und Gegenwart* on the subject of the Enthronement Festival which was never published. In what he wrote Mowinckel had been prepared, in the face of criticisms from Gunkel and others, to modify quite substantially his view, especially as regards the question of the date at which the festival originated. Mowinckel later regretted this temporary yielding to criticism and was pleased that the en-

try never appeared in print, even though this omission was never explained to him.

23. A. Weiser, *Die Psalmen, ausgewählt, übersetzt und erklärt*, Göttingen, 1935; subsequently expanded to include the whole Psalter in the series, *Das Alte Testament Deutsch* (Bd. 14), first edition 1939, fourth edition 1955. English translation by H. Hartwell, *The Psalms. A Commentary*, London, 1962.
24. H. J. Kraus, *Die Königsherrschaft Gottes im Alten Testament*, Beiträge zur historischen Theologie 13, Tübingen, 1951.
25. So especially A. R. Johnson, *Sacral Kingship*, Cardiff, 1955, second edition 1967.
26. Edited by S. H. Hooke, *Myth and Ritual. Essays on the Myth and Ritual of the Hebrews In Relation to the Culture Pattern of the Ancient East*, London, 1933.
27. Edited by S. H. Hooke, *The Labyrinth. Further Studies in the Relation between Myth and Ritual in the Ancient World*, London, 1935.
28. A. R. Johnson, 'The Role of the King in the Jerusalem Cultus,' in *The Labyrinth*, pp. 71–111.
29. H. J. Kraus, especially in *Die Psalmen* (*BKAT* XV), Neukirchen, 1960, pp. 197–205, 'Exkurs 3. Die Kulttraditionen Jerusalems'.
30. I. Engnell, *Studies in Divine Kingship in the Ancient Near East*, Uppsala, 1943, second edition, Oxford, 1967.
31. G. Widengren, *Sakrales Königtum im Alten Testament und im Judentum*, Stuttgart, 1955.
32. A. Bentzen, *Messias-Moses Redivivus-Menschensohn* (*ATANT* 17), Zürich, 1948. English translation *King and Messiah*, first edition, London, 1955; second edition, Oxford, 1970.
33. H. Frankfort, *Kingship and the Gods, A Study of Ancient Near Eastern Religion as the Integration of Society and Nature*, Chicago, 1948.
34. S. Mowinckel, *Han som Kommer*, Copenhagen, 1951. English translation by G. W. Anderson, *He That Cometh*, Oxford, 1956.
35. Beside the work listed above in note 25 A. R. Johnson contributed an essay entitled 'Hebrew Conceptions of Kingship' in *Myth, Ritual and Kingship. Essays on the Theory and Practice of Kingship in the Ancient Near East and in Israel*, edited by S. H. Hooke, Oxford, 1958, pp. 204–235.
36. I. Engnell, *Studies in Divine Kingship in the Ancient Near East* (first edition Uppsala, 1943), second edition, Oxford, 1967, p. 176. Cf. also his article 'The Book of Psalms', *Critical Essays on the Old Testament*, London, 1970, pp. 81ff.
37. H. Schmidt, *Das Gebet der Angeklagten im Alten Testament* (*BZAW* 49), Giessen, 1928.
38. W. Beyerlin, *Die Rettung der Bedrängten in den Feindpsalmen der Einzelnen auf institutionelle Zusammenhänge untersucht* (*FRLANT* 99), Göttingen, 1970.
39. L. Delekat, *Asylie und Schutzorakel am Zionheiligtum. Eine Untersuchung zu den privaten Feindpsalmen*, Leiden, 1967.
40. In *Die Feinde des Individuums in der israelitischen Psalmenliteratur*, Oslo, 1933. Also *The Evildoers in the Book of Psalms*, Oslo, 1955.

41. S. Mowinckel, *The Psalms in Israel's Worship*, Oxford, 1962, Vol. I, pp. 71ff., 225ff.
42. H. Gunkel, 'Nahum I', in *ZAW* 13 (1893), pp. 223–244.
43. H. Gunkel, 'Jesaja 33. Eine prophetische Liturgie', in *ZAW* 42 (1924), pp. 177–208; 'Der Micha-Schluss', *Zeitschrift für Semitistik* 1924, pp. 145–183.
44. H. Gunkel, *Einleitung in die Psalmen*, Göttingen, 1933, pp. 329–381.
45. S. Mowinckel, *Psalmenstudien II*, p. 65.
46. S. Mowinckel, article 'Literature', *The Interpreter's Dictionary of the Bible*, Vol. III, New York and Nashville, 1953, p. 142.
47. S. Mowinckel, *Psalmenstudien III: Kultprophetie und prophetische Psalmen*; Cf. *The Psalms in Israel's Worship*, Vol. II, pp. 53ff.
48. H. Gunkel, *Einleitung in die Psalmen*, pp. 360, 370ff.
49. J. Begrich, *Studien zu Deuterojesaja* (*BWANT* IV: 25), Stuttgart, 1938; reprinted in 1963 under the editorship of W. Zimmerli in the series *Theologische Bücherei* 20, Munich.
50. J. Begrich, 'Das priesterliche Heilsorakel', in *ZAW* 52 (1934), pp. 81–92; reprinted in *Gesammelte Studien zum Alten Testament*, edited by Zimmerli (*Theologische Bücherei* 21), Munich, 1964, pp. 217–231.

6

Interpreting the Wisdom Literature

Within the Old Testament certain books stand apart from the rest on account of their marked didactic character, and a quite distinctive literary style. These are the books of Proverbs, Job and Ecclesiastes which, together with the books of Ecclesiasticus and the Wisdom of Solomon in the Apocrypha, represent the wisdom literature of the Old Testament. Their style and form is unlike that of the prophets, and they include sayings, proverbs, admonitions and exhortations, with little or no specific appeal to explicit laws or commandments. They also display a certain pragmatic cast of thought, which has meant that they have not easily proved capable of being accommodated into the main patterns of interpretation appropriate to the rest of the Old Testament literature. Their literary forms and style are clearly different from the narrative, legal and prophetic forms of speech and writing. Their content also shows a range of interests which are both intensely moral and yet quite unlike the sharp invective of the prophets or the authoritative commandments of the divine law. Furthermore these books show every mark of having reached their present form at a relatively late period of the Old Testament era. All in all they can be readily seen to stand apart, and to have belonged to a distinctive part of ancient Israelite life which necessitates special attention on the part of the scholar who would understand them. At the same time, if their interpretation is to be meaningful it may be expected to show some kind of relationship to that of other parts of the Old Testament literature, so that the setting of wisdom in the overall context of Israel's religious life can be properly seen and evaluated. As a consequence a significant aspect of the interpretation of the wisdom books has been concerned with the problem of relating the distinctive interests and ideas contained in them to the major religious trends of ancient Israel.

In his *Old Testament Theology* H. Schultz, disdaining any very precise critical attempts to date the emergence of wisdom in Israel, argued that it represented a distinctive type of philosophical piety which emerged on the basis of the divine revelation given in the Mosaic law.[1] He claimed that it possessed a religious character from the start, and did not belong to any one particular class of people. Rather it expressed a kind of pious intellectual approach to Israel's revealed religion. For such a viewpoint Schultz appealed to the earlier views of G. F. Oehler. From time to time since then other scholars have sought to find in wisdom a special kind of Israelite philosophical piety, and some apparent plausibility attaches to such a view if attention is concentrated only on the later wisdom writings. Schultz, for example, regarded the dictum 'The fear of Yahweh is the beginning of wisdom' (Proverbs 9:10) as fundamental to all Old Testament wisdom. As a result he thought that this wisdom rested upon the special ideas and values of Yahwism from the outset. Such a view, however, ignored the historical problems about its origins and development in Israel, as they appear in the light of a more critical assessment of the way in which the religion as a whole developed.

In his reconstruction of the course of Israel's religious history, J. Wellhausen paid almost no attention to the wisdom books which he clearly regarded as late and secondary. In part this was no doubt due to the fact that Wellhausen was especially concerned with the history of Israel's religious institutions, and there were no clear indications available to show how wisdom was related to these, nor how their development may have influenced it. B. Duhm, however, in his *Die Theologie der Propheten* of 1875, raised the question of the place at which the teaching found in the book of Proverbs could have arisen in Israel, and the kind of purpose it was intended to serve.[2] From this he introduced into the discussion of wisdom a line of interpretation which has very frequently been applied since. The wise men were regarded as the heirs of the prophets in that they took the great moral principles of justice and of the divine government of the world revealed by the prophets, and applied them to the more mundane and everyday experiences of life. The wise men therefore display an intense moral earnestness, and a deep conviction about the efficacy of divine retribution, which they inherited from the prophets and which they sought to relate to the ordinary conditions of life in Israelite society.

Two points in particular appeared to stand out in this regard as indicative of the dependence of the wise men on the prophets. These were the belief in the certainty of retribution for the wrongdoer and a critical, and predominantly hostile, attitude towards the cult and its claims, especially as it was focused in the rite of sacrifice (cf. Proverbs 15: 8; 21: 27). Certainly the teaching of the book of Proverbs contains a great many allusions to the needs and activities of everyday life in ancient Israel which may appear somewhat trivial when compared with the great issues of the life and death of whole nations proclaimed by the prophets. The sense of the dependence of wisdom on the prophets therefore appeared to be reasonably evidenced as a case of major moral insights being applied to minor situations and cases. In consequence it was felt appropriate by some scholars to see the particular value of the book of Proverbs to lie in the way that its sayings illuminated the concerns and practices of everyday life in ancient Israel.[3] However this belief in the secondary and relatively late emergence of wisdom of Israel was challenged, and in several respects undermined, by two significant developments. The first of these was the application of form, or type, criticism to wisdom sayings, which was initiated by H. Gunkel. The second was the discovery of comparable types of wisdom sayings and poetry among other ancient peoples, especially Egypt and later Babylon.

Gunkel's views regarding the setting of wisdom in Israel are to be found in his sketch of the history of Israelite literature in which he argued that the forms and character of wisdom teaching, especially as exemplified in the book of Proverbs, are so distinctive that they cannot readily be derived from either prophecy or law.[4] They must represent the product of a quite distinctive group within Israel. In fact they must have emanated from a special class of wise men who were concerned with education and man's general progress and advancement in life. Gunkel went on to suggest that this class of wise men, whose special function was that of educators, must have had connections with comparable groups of wise men in other nations and have shared many interests and responsibilities in common with them. Thus wisdom had a markedly international flavour, probably more so than was true of the more specifically religious institutions of Israel.

Although Gunkel accepted that the preserved wisdom writings, including the book of Proverbs, were demonstrably late, he argued that these written products must be distinguished from the oral teaching and collection of wisdom which was very much older, and which must have had roots in the very beginning of Israel's existence as a distinguishable people and culture. Characteristically Gunkel found signs of the lateness of our present collections in their marked note of religious individualism. He distinguished between the older oral wisdom, which had its setting in the teachings of a particular educated class and the later wisdom writings which were more directly religious in their character.

In accordance with his aim of searching for the main lines of literary development within Israel, Gunkel endeavoured to establish the main course of such a development for wisdom. Accepting that the wise men formed a special class, who were primarily concerned with the education of young men from among the wealthier landowners, Gunkel argued that the fundamental form of wisdom instruction was to be found in the brief didactic saying, especially the proverb (Heb. *māshāl* = likeness). Such proverbs were very different in character from modern proverbs, and were designed to discern some pattern, or order, in the moral realm which could be grasped and used to advantage. From this wisdom took on a distinctly worldly character and was pragmatic in its outlook. From such short didactic sayings more extended discourses were developed which came eventually to be written down and to create for themselves new literary styles and forms of their own. On the basis of Gunkel's insights wisdom in the Old Testament undoubtedly took on a new look, for he had been able to show that it had a setting of its own, and was not to be regarded as an extension, or adaptation, of some other branch of instruction or literature. It belonged neither to the cult nor to prophecy, but to a class of people who were to be considered on their own.

Gunkel recognized, as we have noted, that wisdom had an international character, so that Israel's wisdom could be expected to have borrowed from other peoples of the ancient East, especially Egypt and Babylon. He was himself unable, however, to show how and where this had taken place. Soon at least a part of this gap was to be filled in a very dramatic way. As early as 1888 Sir E. W. Budge had brought back from Egypt, along with many other papyri, one which proved on its translation to be an important document of Egyptian moral and religious instruction. This was the Teaching of Amen-em-ope, an important Egyptian official, whose original sayings were here set out in a copy made by a scribe.[5] When a translation of the text was published in 1923 its significance for the study of Old Testament wisdom was quickly recognized. Both in Germany, where H. Gressmann drew attention to it,[6] and Great Britain, where W. O. E. Oesterley wrote about it,[7] its value for the study of the book of Proverbs was immediately seen. The precise date of the Egyptian document was to remain a matter of some uncertainty and discussion, several scholars placing it in the latter half of the second millennium BC, and others allocating it to a date several centuries later. It consisted of general moral instruction, set out in thirty chapters, which were surprising for their markedly religious tone and assumptions. Most striking of all however was the fact that a part of it is reflected so directly in Proverbs 22–24, most directly of all in Proverbs 22: 17–23: 11, that it was impossible to escape the conclusion that some direct relationship exists between the two documents. The simplest explanation is that the Old Testament admonitions have been drawn from a translation of the Egyptian document, although Oesterley suggested that both the Israelite and Egyptian teachings might go back to a common antecedent.[8] In view of the popularity of the Teaching of Amen-em-ope as a didactic text it may even have been that much of it once existed in a Hebrew translation, or even as a bilingual school text.

The consequences of the publication of the Amen-em-ope text were considerable, even though it did not in itself do very much more than confirm what Gunkel had already surmised, that Israel's wisdom teaching had borrowed from that of Egypt. Though even today a number of uncertainties remain about the provenance of the text of Amen-em-ope, its undoubted connection with part of the book of Proverbs serves to indicate in a striking way the international character of wisdom, and the fact that Israelite wisdom must be viewed as a part of this wider pursuit of learning and knowledge. From what had been glimpsed by the connection with the Teaching of Amen-em-ope, a much more widespread indebtedness on Israel's part to the wisdom of the ancient Orient could be regarded as virtually certain. More than this, however, this connection between Israelite and Egyptian moral instruction suggested that the setting of wisdom in Israel might have been very similar to that of Egypt, where a connection with the circle of the court and of wealthier officials and rulers was revealed. Gressmann was able to suggest that the presence of scribes and secretaries in David's court pointed to the kind of persons among whom such a wisdom teaching would have been nursed in Israel.[9] A connection of this kind between the teaching of wisdom and the activities of the royal court, with its responsibilities for the administration of the realm, has in consequence provided a valuable guide into the earliest setting and aims of wisdom teaching in Israel.

In the minds of several scholars it has come to be taken for granted that the court was the natural place at which wisdom would have been nurtured. The concern of several proverbs with the kingship and life at court generally has appeared to confirm this. As a consequence it has been argued by a number of scholars that Solomon, in whose reign Israel's contacts with Egypt were for a time quite close, established a court school of wisdom in Israel. Such however is to go beyond the evidence, and even H. Gressmann's claim, on the basis of the Amen-em-ope text, that we can now accept that the traditions of wisdom teaching in Israel must go back as far as the age of David, has appeared to some scholars a rather speculative one. Admittedly the connections of the book of Proverbs with the Teaching of Amen-em-ope do not amount to proof of this, and do no more than suggest that it is a possibility. Nevertheless certain general inferences about Israelite wisdom have been rendered very probable in the light of the Amen-em-ope discovery. That the teaching of wisdom was the aim of a particular school, or schools, and that such teaching was at one time closely associated with the royal court and the processes of governmental administration appear likely. Furthermore the distinctively international character of wisdom has been decisively confirmed.

Even in the light of these discoveries no evidence had been produced to weigh against the claim that our present book of Proverbs is a post-exilic work and that it bears the marks of its relatively late origin in many of its literary and stylistic features as well as in some aspects of the character of its ethical teaching. What had now become evident was that a substantial dimension of historical depth lay within the book, so that we can in no way assume that all its contents arose close to the age of its main author or editor. Such a view, with its implicit recognition of the kind of traditio-historical analyses advocated by Gunkel in other areas of the Old Testament literature, was now firmly vindicated and eagerly taken up by H. Gressmann. So far as the date at which wisdom began to be taught and encouraged in Israel was concerned what was significant in the new discoveries was not that there were now reasons for assigning a much earlier date to the book of Proverbs, but rather that a very long history of wisdom instruction could be discerned to lie within the book. This may well have had its origin as far back as the age of Solomon, even though it was difficult to adduce workable criteria by which early wisdom compositions could be identified.

In a larger context the recognition that a connection existed between Israel's wisdom teaching and that of Egypt has served to illustrate a wider feature of the interpretation of the Old Testament which appears all the clearer in retrospect. It was fundamental to the conclusions reached by Wellhausen and Duhm regarding the historical development of Israel's religion that the revelatory character of the Old Testament, and in consequence its abiding worth for mankind, lay in its close binding together of religion and morality. 'Ethical monotheism' became a kind of catchphrase by which the truly distinctive character of the Old Testament, and its significance for mankind's religious development, was thought to be defined. The sources of this intensely moral understanding of religion were traced to the prophets, beginning with Amos, who were regarded as the pioneers of a new awareness that only in morality, a proper regard for social justice and a human striving after righteousness, could the will of God be done. The moral insights presupposed in the laws of the Old Testament, and the ethical basis of the instruction urged upon the young in the wisdom writings, were both regarded as derivative from this prophetic revelation of the primacy of moral understanding for religion. Yet already in the discovery of the law code of Hammurabi at the end of the nineteenth century, and the recognition of its relationship, even though somewhat distant, to the laws of the Old Testament, the fact was beginning to be made incontrovertably clear that morality had not suddenly been discovered by Israel in the eighth century BC. On the contrary some awareness of man's moral duties, and of the importance attaching to his obligations in society, belonged to the very dawn of civilization and the emergence of the city-state. The more information that was obtained about the origin and development of civilization in ancient Mesopotamia and Egypt the more evident it was becoming that they also had been forced to deal with fundamental problems of morality, such as had later faced Israel. There was no simple 'discovery' of morality which had passed on from one civilization to another like an olympic torch. The recognition of an element of Israelite indebtedness in its tradition of education to similar traditions in Egypt brought further confirmation of this.

The discovery of the connection between the wisdom of the book of Proverbs and the Teaching of Amen-em-ope provided an excellent illustration of this changing realization. It offered an important starting point for the whole question of the origin of morality and of man's ethical consciousness, and this was taken up by J. H. Breasted in his book *The Dawn of Conscience* in 1933.[10] He referred to the fresh light from the Teaching of Amen-em-ope as a 'most extraordinary revelation', and sought in his study to draw a broad sketch of the existence of man's moral insight and concern for social justice in Egypt long before the time of Moses. Throughout he was very conscious of the fact that he had been brought up to believe that the basic insights of morality had first been revealed to the ancient Hebrews and had been handed on by them to mankind. He recounts in his preface,

> I had more disquieting experiences before me, when as a young orientalist I found that the Egyptians had possessed a standard of morals far superior to that of the Decalogue over a thousand years before the Decalogue was written (pp. xi–xii).

In his book Breasted was then able to proceed to demonstrate without difficulty how ancient Egypt had developed a social conscience, and had become aware of the importance of individual responsibility and of the necessity of a moral order in society. He saw in Egypt evidence of what almost amounted to a crusade for social justice and for what he termed 'the democratization of moral responsibility'. In a concluding chapter he was able to show how wide ranging are the sources of our moral heritage, in which he claimed that a very special place of eminence lay with ancient Egypt.

For the student of the Old Testament the various details of Breasted's study are less significant than the overall impact of the picture which he was able to draw of man's moral history. The rise of a critical historical study of the Old Testament had attached immense importance to the novelty of the demand for social justice found in the eighth century prophets and to the deepened sense of the moral claims of religion revealed in the prophets more generally. Scholars had come to claim that these prophets had pointed to truths which had not previously been known to man, and which by themselves fully justified their claim to be proclaiming a revelation from God. What was thought to be new in the prophets was identified with their attacks against all forms of immorality and social injustice. Although Breasted's study displays a rather partisan spirit in its regard for the virtues of ancient Egyptian civilization, it was nevertheless symptomatic of a gradual crumbling away of some of the edifices built up by Old Testament scholars in defending the uniquely revealed character of Israel's religion.

It is clear, even upon a superficial acquaintance, that Old Testament wisdom is related to the ethics of the Old Testament in a particularly close way. The element of admonition and ethical advice is very prominent in it whilst the themes concerning Israel's divine election and destiny, which are more evident in the historical and prophetic books, are almost entirely absent. Yet it was proving extremely difficult for scholarship to give clear indications how and why this ethical element in Israelite wisdom was different from the patterns of moral behaviour to be found elsewhere in the ancient East. The very fact that wisdom teachers appealed to their hearers and readers simply as men, and not as Israelites in a special relationship of covenant or election with God, shows how the moral guidance given by wisdom differed from the religious assumptions of the Old Testament laws. Their moral insight could not readily be shown to be fundamentally dependent either upon Israel's traditions of law, or upon the preaching of the prophets. In relation to this observation it is, perhaps, appropriate to note that the subject of Old Testament ethics has proved to be a most difficult one to deal with, and has in fact generally been treated as a subsidiary part of the wider study of Old Testament theology. The literature devoted to it has been surprisingly sparse, and the complex interaction of historical, sociological and religious factors has made it a subject in which it has been difficult to avoid the merely superficial.

The evidence that Israel's wisdom was related to a wider context of similar teaching in the ancient East, especially in Egypt, provided a particular example of a truth that was rapidly becoming clearer; that at a great many points, in its cultus, political organization and general cultural achievement, Israel had shared fully in the life of the ancient East. There were nevertheless differences in Israel, which had to be recognized and explained. Just as this was evident in the whole range of Israel's religious life, so also could it be expected to be true of wisdom. What made this area of Israel's cultural development especially interesting was the rich evidence of the international context in which it had taken place, and the striking fact that the wisdom writings lacked the more obviously distinctive features concerning Israel's divine election and the history in which this destiny had been discerned. So far as the study of wisdom was concerned two scholars in particular, J. Fichtner[11] and J. C. Rylaarsdam,[12] directed their attention to this problem, the first of them very consciously in the aftermath of the discovery of the connection between the Teaching of Amen-em-ope and the book of Proverbs.

Fichtner started out from the clear recognition that Israel's wisdom, like that of the ancient orient generally, was eudaemonistic in character and had begun as a development of a wider concern for obtaining a mastery of life through reflection and the handing on of this in the form of admonitions and instructions. Fichtner argued that we must clearly hold apart in our minds this older wisdom of Israel from that of later

Judaism, which had recognizably absorbed much of the very distinctive piety centred upon the *torah*, or law, contained in a written tradition. This later wisdom was clearly to be seen in the teaching of Ben Sira in Ecclesiasticus. Fichtner's concern therefore was twofold in its aim, for he not only sought to show how wisdom had developed in Israel from its early pragmatic form into something very different, but also to show how the earliest wisdom had itself acquired a distinctively Israelite character. In many respects the latter was the more difficult task since it entailed making a distinction in the book of Proverbs between the earlier and the later material. In the oldest wisdom teaching Fichtner noted the ways in which the understanding of the activity of God was affected by the particular Israelite notions of Yahweh. Israelite wisdom knew of only one God, Yahweh, who effected retribution in accordance with his own all-embracing justice. As a consequence the religious element enters more directly into the moral sphere through the close connection of the idea of moral retribution with the belief in a divine power working immanently in the world to uphold justice. Furthermore, in spite of this religious element, the sphere of the cult plays almost no role in the teaching of the wise men, a fact which Fichtner attributed to the markedly anti-cultic bias which developed in Israel's piety. Thus, without in any way denying or undervaluing the general oriental context in which Israelite wisdom emerged, Fichtner was able to argue that there were many features in it which showed the influence of Israel's own unique religious experience. As a result wisdom had grown up in Israel into a quite distinctively Israelite phenomenon.

Although it stands somewhat apart from the main lines of interest which developed in the wake of the Amen-em-ope discovery, we may mention here the work of H. Ranston, whose study *Ecclesiastes and Early Greek Wisdom Literature*[13] considered the distinctive teaching of one of the Old Testament wisdom books from a very different standpoint. Ranston's thesis was that there were significant points of connection between the teaching to be found in the book of Ecclesiastes and the older Greek gnomic sayings and aphorisms. These contacts fell short of demonstrating a clear dependence, but they did suggest that there were signs of some common tradition behind both spheres of teaching. In the light of the much fuller understanding of the deep roots of moral instruction and admonition which is now evident from numerous texts found in Mesopotamia and Egypt, and which constitutes a kind of ancient oriental wisdom tradition, the ancestry of such gnomic teaching is scarcely to be doubted.

However it was the American scholar J. C. Rylaarsdam who took up again the problem of the uniqueness of Israelite wisdom in the light of its international origins in his book *Revelation in Jewish Wisdom Literature*. Rylaarsdam's starting point was the recognition of a confidently pragmatic outlook which is to be discerned in the earliest Israelite wisdom which assumed throughout that man could master life if he used his intellectual gifts to search out truth. A basic assumption of the early wisdom was the conviction that man could readily find wisdom if he diligently sought after it. Such a conviction amounted to a belief in a kind of natural revelation of truth about the order of the universe which man could discover by his use of the gifts with which God had endowed him. In the later Jewish wisdom teaching, however, as is well exemplified by the book of Ecclesiasticus, the path which man had to tread in order to find wisdom was conceived very differently. In this writing wisdom is identified with the teaching of the Mosaic law, which had been uniquely given to Israel in the past by an act of divine revelation, and was to be accepted by man in an act of piety and faith (Ecclus. 24: 8ff.). In this case wisdom was regarded as the object of an act of special divine disclosure, which man could never have discovered by his own unaided searching. It was a gift from God. Rylaarsdam's concern was to trace the course of this development, which had resulted in such a marked change in the conception of the revelation of wisdom.[14]

Looked at from one point of view it is clear that this concern with the understanding of revelation was a further aspect of the problem concerning the adoption of wisdom into Israel, and the way in which wisdom had, as a consequence, absorbed elements of Israelite-Jewish religion. In the outcome, in spite of some interesting points of connection with Greek gnomic instruction, this development resulted in the growth of a form of Jewish intellectual piety which was highly distinctive. It had nevertheless sufficient points of connection with the oriental and Hellenistic worlds to provide a central basis of apologetic and intellectual appeal by which Jews could uphold and spread their faith. In Judaism both the central emphasis upon the law as a source of guidance for the whole of life, and the growing tendency towards a practical separation from the temple worship, fostered a deepened interest in wisdom and its appropriation.

The recognition of the connection between Israelite and Egyptian wisdom brought a new dimension to the origins of wisdom in Israel both by suggesting a very much earlier date for its emergence than had previously been supposed and also by pointing to a possible source for such a development. This was the royal court, for there were clearly a number of circumstantial reasons for thinking of this as the place where wisdom was nurtured in Israel, just as a comparable type of instruction had belonged to the court circles of Egypt. Israelite tradition itself pointed to such a connection by its ascription of wisdom in considerable measure to Solomon, which had in any case clearly been an age when contacts with Egypt were closer than at any other time during the Old Testament period.

Although the ancient Egyptian instructional sayings did not contain any one word or expression which could provide an exact counterpart to the Hebrew term for wisdom, the general didactic and educational interest of several Egyptian writings left no doubt that they were a true part of the intellectual heritage of Israelite wisdom. Amen-em-ope himself was an important Egyptian official, and his concern in his teaching was to pass on what he had learnt for its moral worth and also for its guidance for those who, like himself, were burdened with responsibility. H. Gressmann suggested that Solomon's court marked the place where wisdom was introduced into Israel and that it too, like its Egyptian prototype, was concerned with the education of government officials as a privileged professional class.[15] The belief that such a court wisdom school was introduced into Israel in Solomon's time has since gained wide currency among Old Testament scholars. It has been suggested that the list of government officials given in I Kings 4: 2ff. points to the leading administrative offices which would have required a body of professionally trained wise men.[16] Varying aspects of such a hypothesis have attracted the attention of scholars, although as an attempt to account for the emergence of wisdom in Israel it combines together a number of separate claims of varying probability.

As far as the broad general claim is concerned, that the age of Solomon witnessed a remarkable opening up of Israel's cultural horizons, especially towards Egypt, there can be little cause for doubt. The particular functions of the Solomonic officers and the explicit evidence of Solomon's marriage with an Egyptian princess all point in this direction. Many aspects of the structure and organization of the Israelite state indicate a substantial measure of dependence on Egyptian prototypes. There is good reason therefore for holding that wisdom gained a distinctive foothold in Israel as a result of these developments. What is less clear is the extent to which wisdom in Israel remained tied to a particular class or professional group within the nation, and the degree to which it remained primarily concerned with the education of government officials. W. McKane has argued that the basic aims and assumptions of wisdom show a direct connection with the needs of political administrators,[17] but recognizes that the evidence of the wisdom instruction and teaching that has been preserved shows a much wider application to the problems of right action in everyday life. At some stage therefore the scope of wisdom was broadened out so that it ceased to be primarily the expertise of government officials and concerned itself with the problems of living which faced everyman. Whilst it is impossible to reconstruct a chronology of such a development in Israel, there are no reasons for ruling out the possibility that such a process of re-moulding of wisdom began in Solomon's age itself, or soon afterwards. This point is important in view of the claims made that early wisdom in Israel was essentially eudaemonistic and 'profane' in its outlook.

Whatever the situation in Egypt, it is not clear that this was the case in Israel and that wisdom did not from the start of its transplantation into its new religious environment adopt many of the fundamental assumptions of the latter. In fact it seems very probable that some adjustment of this kind became necessary from the beginning so that we do not need to look for any special crisis in the history of wisdom in Israel in order to account for it. Furthermore the questions of the relationship between wisdom and the court, and the connection of this with a school of wisdom, have been raised as a result of several features in the content of proverbial sayings and admonitions. That the king figures surprisingly often in such sayings points in this direction, and, if not always flattering to him, such sayings are in no way critical of the monarchy as an institution. So far as the existence of a specific wisdom school in Israel is concerned however, and the immediate aims of the wise men, the impression created by our book of Proverbs is of a concern to teach young men in general, rather than to educate a professional élite. The atmosphere breathed by the book is that of a landowning middle class, with time for leisure and reflection, rather than that of a more narrowly confined court, or government, circle. Perhaps even more important is the recognition that the more directly practical skills of translators, writers, secretaries, accountants, lawyers and archivists, all so necessary for the effective working of government, are not explicitly the subjects which interest the wise men. The impression is given that such practical skills, which are much more likely than broader moral questions to have been taught in specific guilds or schools, were left to people of more junior rank than the wise men considered themselves to

111

be. In this respect it is of importance that the Teaching of Amen-em-ope consists of a secretary's record of what the revered official had taught.

Overall therefore we may note that the claim that a strong connection existed between wisdom and the court in Israel breaks down into a number of further questions. In general such a claim must be upheld, but many of the supporting hypotheses which have been related to it are more questionable. There is no evidence that Solomon founded a specific school of wisdom in Jerusalem, although it is probable that the opening up of relationships with Egypt during this king's reign provided the cultural opportunity for the entry of a sophisticated type of wisdom into Israel. Nor are we justified in assuming that the primary aim of wisdom was the training of suitable government officials, since the content of our present book of Proverbs can scarcely substantiate this.

The question of the effect upon wisdom of its implanting into Israel has been a subject which has especially concerned the German scholar G. von Rad. First in a brief sketch included in the first volume of his *Old Testament Theology*,[18] and then much more extensively in a volume devoted entirely to the subject,[19] von Rad has examined the religious assumptions and significance of Israelite wisdom. The title of this latter volume, *Wisdom in Israel*, adequately shows the author's concern to examine the consequences of what it meant for Israel to participate in the quest for wisdom, of which we find evidence more widely throughout the ancient east.

The basic starting point for von Rad is that wisdom was experiential in its method of working and sought to fathom the order which lies within and behind the universe, so that man may master life. Hence wisdom presupposed a belief in the existence of order in the world, which man could perceive and use to his advantage, and it endeavoured to formulate rules or norms pertaining to this order, by which man's conduct could be regulated. In Israel the order of the universe was necessarily perceived in religious terms through the nation's belief in its relationship to Yahweh and its deep conviction that its destiny had been established by its encounter with him. From this von Rad recognizes that a religious dimension attached even to the earliest Israelite wisdom since the world in which the Israelite lived was one in which the existence and activity of Yahweh was fully accepted. It is wrong therefore to think of Israel's wisdom as being essentially 'secular' or 'profane'. On the contrary it was concerned with the divine realm very directly since it was believed that every Israelite encountered the divine order in the normal course of his life.

A prominent feature of von Rad's exposition of what was distinctive about wisdom in Israel is his attempt to show that it was concerned to define the limits of man's ability to master his life and that it was interested in marking off the areas of life which properly belong to Yahweh alone. For this interest von Rad points to such sayings as Proverbs 16: 1, 2, 9 and 19: 14, 21, which reveal an awareness of an element of incalculability in man's conduct of his affairs. Not every event can be foreseen, and the ultimate outcome of each human decision and action makes necessary a recognition of the limitations imposed by God upon man's government of his life. A true humility towards him is essential therefore, expressed in a reverent submission to his will which must be recognized as reaching far beyond the range of man's own knowledge. In this way von Rad was able to point to a theological dimension which belonged to the earliest wisdom in Israel, but which did not deny its practical and prudential character since it presupposed both. Such a saying as 'The fear of Yahweh is the beginning of knowledge' (Proverbs 9: 10) does not represent a late theological importation into a fundamentally secular and pragmatic expertise, but rather belonged to wisdom from a very early stage.

On the basis of these observations about the implanting of wisdom in Israel von Rad went on to point to a fundamentally altered conception of reality, which stood over against what he described as the 'pansacralism' of the earliest period of Israel's existence. The key to understanding this development he found in the changed intellectual climate of Solomon's era in which the adoption of wisdom into Israel had been a major contributing factor. The further effects of this new intellectual approach to religion led to the acquisition by wisdom of a totally new and distinctively Israelite character, which led it out of the more narrowly restrictive confines of its earlier pragmatism. At the same time its effect on Israel's religion was quite profound in that it affirmed a new questioning attitude which challenged the older assumptions of the cult and led to a more genuinely theological interpretation of religion.

One quite distinctive and unexpected area in which von Rad saw the influence of wisdom emerging was in that of early Jewish apocalyptic. Where previously scholars had been almost unanimous in agreeing that apocalyptic grew up as a child of prophecy this claim was now fundamentally contested by von Rad. It is impossible, von Rad argued, to regard apocalyptic as deriving from prophecy by any kind of direct connection. Their basic assumptions are so diverse, for prophecy is concerned with the foretelling, and interpretation, of the future as a natural continuation of the historical process out of the present. Apocalyptic on the other hand works with a conception of fixed ages, and is concerned with what lies beyond history, rather than with the next step within it. It is then no accident that Daniel, the hero of the earliest extant Jewish apocalypse, is described as a wise man and exemplifies many of the characteristic virtues and ideals of Jewish wisdom. Von Rad drew special attention to the understanding of history in apocalyptic as standing in marked contrast to that of prophecy. He argued that its notion of ages, standing in a predetermined sequence and coloured by an overriding characterization as good or evil, arose out of the wisdom belief that there is a time for everything (Ecclesiastes 3: 1ff.). While the awareness of a genuine wisdom influence upon apocalyptic has aroused considerable interest, von Rad's sharp separation of it from prophecy has encountered criticism and opposition, and the further examination of such an interesting hypothesis must be regarded as still in progress.

The recognition that Israelite wisdom was to some extent indebted to, and an offshoot of, the educational and literary interest of the ancient Near East generally has led to a marked concentration upon those aspects of Old Testament wisdom which link it with the sophisticated world of the royal court and the wealthier classes. Yet from the outset it has also been noted by scholars of all kinds that, alongside the more consciously aesthetic and intellectual features of wisdom, there were also aspects of it which belonged to the simple family life of ordinary people. The popularity of such artistic forms of speech as the parable, the fable, the allegory and various other skilful or humorous types of saying among all kinds of people, both rustic and urban, shows that there are basic elements of wisdom which belong to all types of community life. They are not limited to the court or the middle classes. They must therefore undoubtedly have had a currency in Israel long before the time of Solomon, and before any strong influence was felt by Israel from the more advanced civilizations of Egypt or Mesopotamia. To speak of borrowing in such a context would be radically misleading, since all types and classes of people may invent and appropriate such compositions. Thus alongside the more developed wisdom of Israel, with its particular colouring and background, there were other elements of wisdom which must be regarded as representing a part of the old folk heritage of Israel's life. Such folk wisdom sayings would have been concerned with the education of the young, especially the young men, of the clans and tribes, although learners of all ages would certainly have listened to, and benefited from, such teaching.

While the existence of such a folk wisdom in Israel has never seriously been denied, its presence has often tended to be overlooked, and it is very much to the credit of E. Gerstenberger[20] and H. W. Wolff[21] to have drawn fresh attention to it. Gerstenberger presented his findings in connection with his study of the Decalogue, with its distinctive mandatory, or apodictic, form of injunction, which had so caught the attention of A. Alt. However, whereas Alt had sought to trace the origin of such a form to the cult, in which an authorized priestly spokesman issued such commandments on the basis of his divine authority, Gerstenberger argued that the origin of such a form was to be found in clan life, where the chief, or father, instructed the young men of the clan. He claimed that the original authority which such commandments presupposed was that of the clan, voiced through its leader, and only secondarily was this authority subsumed into the wider religious authority of the cult. Gerstenberger sought to show that parallels to such 'folk wisdom' injunctions were to be found in references to clan teaching, and he pointed especially to the example of the sons of Jonadab-ben-Rechab in Jeremiah 35: 6–10. In this way the older, and more popular, stratum of wisdom, which had grown up in the unsophisticated life of the clans and tribes of old Israel, was seen by Gerstenberger as the place where the apodictic form and the moral urgency to be found in the Decalogue were originally at home.

H. W. Wolff's interest in such old folk wisdom emerged quite directly out of his studies of prophecy, and especially of the book of Amos. We have already had occasion to note the way in which Wolff became critical of the attempts on the part of scholars to trace the background of the forms of prophetic speech of this book, and many of its leading themes, to the cult. At the same time scholars had abandoned the view that wisdom was largely to be regarded as an adaptation to everyday life of the moral teaching of the prophets. In consequence the possibility could no longer be ruled out that the prophets had in fact been influenced from traditions of wisdom. Such a claim was put forward by S. Terrien in the case of Amos,[22] and by J. Lindblom with a somewhat wider references.[23] In looking at the particular intellectual background of Amos, H. W. Wolff discovered this to lie particularly in the realm of the older folk wisdom. It was of special importance to Wolff to show that what we find in Amos is not the kind of developed wisdom such as we have come to associate with the court with its international milieu, but the older moral instruction which belonged to the more rural and unsophisticated areas of Israel.

The developments in the interpretation of wisdom in the Old Testament have proved to be among the most striking of all the branches of its literature. The earliest phase of critical study found no clear literary or historical features by which to locate it firmly in a particular place of its own in Israel's life. As a consequence the general conviction was expressed that, as an intellectual movement, wisdom must be placed late in the sequence of Israel's religious and moral developmer:. It was therefore ascribed to a position and date after the prophets and the law, although standing close to the latter. The recovery of a knowledge of the didactic and instructional literature of ancient Egypt and Mesopotamia, however, has revealed a rich wealth of compositions which can clearly be seen to be related to the wisdom books of the Old Testament. In this light Israel's wisdom can be seen to be a part of an old, and strikingly international, intellectual enterprise. In such a fresh light the study of wisdom has come to enjoy a quite new place in Old Testament studies in which it can be recognized as a significant source of intellectual and theological vitality. The need has arisen to show, so far as is possible, what was distinctive of wisdom in its specifically Israelite dress, and to explore the ways in which it exercised an influence on various areas of Israel's life: its political organization, its traditions of law, history-writing and prophecy. In these areas several valuable avenues of interpretation have been suggested, but have not yet been fully investigated.

1. H. Schultz, *Old Testament Theology*, Vol. II, Edinburgh, 1898, pp. 83–6.
2. B. Duhm, *Die Theologie der Propheten*, Bonn, 1875, pp. 244–5.
3. Cf. W. A. L. Elmslie, *Studies in Life from Jewish Proverbs*, London, 1917.
4. H. Gunkel, 'Die Israelitische Literatur', in *Die Kultur der Gegenwart*, edited by P. Hinneberg, Berlin and Leipzig, 1906, p. 90.
5. F. Ll. Griffith, 'The Teaching of Amenophis. The Son of Kanakht. Papyrus BM10474', *Journal of Egyptian Archaeology* 12 (1925), pp. 191–231. A. Erman, 'Eine ägyptische Quelle der Sprüche Salomos', *Sitzungsberichte der preussischen Akademie der Wissenschaften zu Berlin, Phil. Hist. Klasse* xv (1914), pp. 86–93.
6. H. Gressmann, 'Die neugefundene Lehre des Amen-em-ope und die vorexilische Spruchdichtung Israels', in *ZAW* 42 (1924), pp. 272–296. The text was first published and translated by E. A. Wallis Budge, *Egyptian Hieratic Papyri in the British Museum*, Second series, London, 1923.
7. W. O. E. Oesterley, *The Wisdom of Egypt and the Old Testament in the Light of the Newly Discovered Teaching of Amenemope*, London, 1927. Cf. 'The Teaching of Amenemope and the Old Testament,' in *ZAW* 45 (1927), pp. 9–24.

8. W. O. E. Oesterley, *The Wisdom of Egypt and the Old Testament*, pp. 98ff.

9. H. Gressmann, *op. cit.*, pp. 280ff.

10. J. H. Breasted, *The Dawn of Conscience*, New York and London, 1933.

11. J. Fichtner, *Die altorientalische Weisheit in ihrer israelitisch-jüdischen Ausprägung. Eine Studie zur Nationalisierung der Weisheit in Israel* (*BZAW* 62), 1933.

12. J. C. Rylaarsdam, *Revelation in Jewish Wisdom Literature*, Chicago, 1944.

13. H. Ranston, *Ecclesiastes and Early Greek Wisdom Literature*, London, 1925.

14. J. C. Rylaarsdam, *op. cit.*, esp. pp. 30ff.

15. H. Gressmann, *op. cit.*, p. 280.

16. So especially in the thesis by the Swedish scholar, T. N. D. Mettinger, *Solomonic State Officials. A Study of the Civil Government Officials of the Israelite Monarchy* (Coniectanea Biblica 5), Lund, 1971.

17. W. Mckane, *Prophets and Wise Men* (*SBT* 44), London, 1965. Cf. also his commentary *Proverbs. A New Approach*, London, 1970.

18. G. von Rad, *Old Testament Theology*, Vol. 1, Edinburgh, 1962, pp. 418–452.

19. G. von Rad, *Weisheit in Israel*, Neukirchen-Vluyn, 1970. English translation by J. D. Martin, *Wisdom in Israel*, London, 1972.

20. E. Gerstenberger, *Wesen und Herkunft des 'apodiktischen Rechts'*, (*WMANT* 20), Neukirchen-Vluyn, 1965. Cf. also his essay 'Covenant and Commandment', in *JBL* 84 (1965), pp. 38–51.

21. So especially in his study *Amos the Prophet. The Man and his Background*, Philadelphia, 1973.

22. S. Terrien, 'Amos and Wisdom'. *Israel's Prophetic Heritage*, edited by B. W. Anderson and W. Harrelson, London, 1962, pp. 108–115.

23. J. Lindblom, 'Wisdom in the Old Testament Prophets', in *Wisdom in Israel and the Ancient Near East*, edited by M. Noth and D. Winton Thomas (Supplements to *Vetus Testamentum* III), Leiden, 1955, pp. 192–204.

7

Interpreting Old Testament Theology

Although J. Wellhausen did not write any significant essay or book on the subject of Old Testament theology, his researches into the history of Israel's religion contained very far-reaching theological comment. Thus in his brief sketch of Israel written for the *Encyclopedia Britannica* he incorporated into a summary of the work of the eighth century prophets insights regarding the overall achievement of Israelite religion and an assessment of why, among the religions of the ancient world, that of Israel made a unique and lasting contribution to mankind. This was uniquely concerned with the work of the canonical prophets and their interpretation of events which they foretold, commencing with Amos:

> The prophets of Israel alone did not allow themselves to be taken by surprise by what had occurred, or to be plunged in despair; they solved by anticipation the given problem which history placed before them. They absorbed into their religion that conception of the world which was destroying the religions of the nations, even before it had been fully grasped by the secular consciousness. Where others saw only the ruin of everything that is holiest, they saw the triumph of Jehovah over delusion and error. Whatever else might be overthrown, the really worthy remained unshaken. They recognized ideal powers only, right and wrong, truth and falsehood; second causes were matters of indifference to them, they were no practical politicians.[1]

> The ethical element destroyed the national character of the old religion. It still addressed itself, to be sure, more to the nation and to society at large than to the individual; it insisted less upon a pure heart than upon righteous institutions; but nevertheless the first step towards universalism had been accomplished, towards at once the general diffusion and the individualization of religion. Thus, although the prophets were far from originating a new conception of God, they none the less were the founders of what has been

called 'ethical monotheism'. The downfall of the nations did not take place until the truths and precepts of religion were already strong enough to be able to live on alone; to the prophets belongs the merit of having recognized the independence of these, and of having secured perpetuity to Israel by refusing to allow the conception of Jehovah to be involved in the ruin of the kingdom. They saved faith by destroying illusion.[2]

These quotations show very clearly the importance which Wellhausen attached to the realm of religious ideas, 'the truths and precepts of religion', and demonstrate how he conceived such ideas to have arisen in Israel's history, originally in a particular context of events, but subsequently becoming isolated and preserved in their own right. Wellhausen saw it as vital to his task as a historian to recognize the emergence of these religious ideas in their proper setting, although it was also clearly a possible procedure to set them apart, and to treat them as an independent subject of examination in the Old Testament. To do this however was to run the risk of reducing these ideas to abstraction by cutting them loose from the situations in which their own worth and significance had become sharply apparent. In Wellhausen's view the historical development of Israel's religion was conceived as having given rise to certain fundamental religious ideas, focusing primarily upon 'ethical monotheism', and these ideas were regarded as constituting the content of divine revelation in the Old Testament.

From the new critical standpoint which Wellhausen established there emerged one work in particular which set out to be a *Biblical Theology of the Old Testament*. This was by B. Stade, the first, and only, volume of which was published in 1905.[3] However, once the contents are examined it is clear that what Stade offers is in fact a historical survey of the development of Israel's religion, with no clear attempt to distinguish the methods appropriate to the latter from that of a theological treatment. The work divides the religion into two main epochs: that of the preprophetic religion and that of the religion as reformed by the prophets from the time of Amos. For the rest the presentation adheres to the general assessments affirmed by Wellhausen, with no serious attempt to isolate the religious ideas from the institutional and cultic life in which they were set.

From a slightly earlier period, however, and from a much more conservative and pietistic standpoint, there already existed in German an influential work on the theology of the Old Testament. This was by H. Schultz, whose two volume work dates from 1869.[4] It is set out in two major divisions, thereby drawing attention to a particular difficulty inherent in any attempt to set out an Old Testament theology, and establishing a precedent which several other scholars have found it convenient to follow in attempting the same task. The first division of Schultz's work sets out 'The Development of Religion and Morals' in the Old Testament, and does this by means of a chronologically ordered account of the major phases of religious development reflected in the literature, showing how the great theological and ethical ideas arose in relation to particular institutions and events. The second division attempts a systematic treatment of these ideas in their interrelationship under the somewhat cumbersome title 'Israel's Consciousness of Salvation and Religious View of the World, the Product of the Religious History of the People'. This section endeavoured to combine together the major ideas under the broad designations of Israel's communion with God, its view of man and the world and the prophetic hope.

In terms of systematizing the great variety of ideas present in the Old Testament Schultz's work was remarkably perceptive and skilful. It worked, so far as is possible, within the terminology of the Old Testament, and laid down a certain precedence and order between concepts and ideas which are seldom consciously related in this way in the Old Testament. The consequence of this is to present the reader with a faith that is much more self-conscious and philosophically reflective than the Old Testament literature appears at first glance to warrant. Futher the nature and intention of the individual documents of the Old Testament are set aside in deference to the need to cull from them a host of varied inferences necessary towards the reconstruction of a systematic account of the theological ideas of ancient Israel. The skill of the theologian is made to compensate for the historical fact that ancient Israel did not itself systematize its faith in this way. Nevertheless Schultz, like Wellhausen although with many different emphases, regarded these ideas as the supreme achievement of the Old Testament. For him the presentation of an Old Testament theology was essentially a systematic account of the religious ideas of ancient Israel for which the Old Testament literature served as a vehicle of communication. The critically minded historian could sift this literature and place it in its proper chronological sequence so that the genesis of the ideas could be recognized and understood. Seen in this light the historico-critical approach to the Old Testament was regarded as a step towards facilitating the recovery of the fundamental theological ideas which had emerged in ancient Israel.

In Schultz's work the reader becomes conscious of a strongly apologetic motive so that, although the traditional Christian interpretations of the Old Testament as a book of prophetic promise and messianic predictions about the coming of Jesus Christ are abandoned, there is nonetheless a firm moral apologetic. Israel's religion is superior to that of all other ancient (or modern non-Christian) religions, making it a fundamental groundwork to Christianity, so that 'an Old Testament saint did not need to change his religion in order to become a Christian.'[5] Schultz regarded only three religions as worthy to be compared with that of the Old Testament, viz. the religions of Persia, Buddhism and Islam, and he had no difficulty in claiming that even these were considerably inferior. Like Wellhausen, Schultz betrayed a totally inadequate awareness of the closeness of the connections between the Israelite religion and that of Canaan, and through this with other older religions of Mesopotamia.

In process of time the spade of the archaeologist and the skill of the linguist in deciphering ancient scripts were to show that the line between the religion of revelation and those of heathenism was no easy one to draw. At a great many points what has been claimed as the unique achievement of the Old Testament can be seen in retrospect to have been based upon a false, or inadequately formulated, contrast between the Old Testament and its background. In particular the sharp demarcation between the religious ideas of the Old Testament and the religious life of the ancient East can be seen to have projected into the study of the Old Testament a conscious isolation of its religious ideas from the life and activities in which they emerged which the evidence scarcely warrants.

Even so Schultz's achievement was an interesting one, and obtained a wide popularity. It serves very well to highlight problems which have continued to beset the Old Testament theologian in the twentieth century. His twofold presentation of the material, one historical and one systematic, in particular has appealed to several other scholars as a convenient method of approach. Hence we find a comparable twofold presentation in the work of E. Sellin in 1932, who divided his study between a history of Israel's religion and an Old Testament theology.[6] The distinction between the historical development of the religion and the faith of the Israelite-Jewish people has appeared valuable as a means of overcoming so much of the historical particularism of the Old Testament. The former is taken to be concerned with religious institutions and the latter with ideas about God and man which have a more timeless significance. Whereas the modern Christian can in no way see

121

himself as related to, or involved in, the religious and cultic life of ancient Israel, which must necessarily remain remote from us, he can, so Schultz and Sellin believed, nevertheless appropriate to himself the fundamental ideas of this religion. O. Procksch too, in a work which was published posthumously in 1951, and which takes on an enhanced significance because Procksch was the teacher of Eichrodt, advocated a similar twofold division of the material of an Old Testament theology, one section being historical and the other systematic.[7]

The convenience and usefulness of such a twofold division is evident. It enables us to preserve a recognition of the historical context in which the religious ideas emerged, while at the same time it makes it possible for us to separate them from this context in order to treat them systematically. Nevertheless the very convenience of such a division serves in the long run to emphasize, rather than to resolve, the fundamental problem created by trying to study Israel's religious ideas in abstraction. Israel itself did not make such a separation of the intellectual side of its religion, and to do so in a modern systematic study draws attention to it in a way which is uncharacteristic of the religious life in which it originally functioned. Nowhere does the Old Testament literature offer a presentation of Israel's theological ideas in abstraction, nor does it claim that they are the most vital and abiding features of its life. The Old Testament does not define worship of Yahweh in terms of accepting certain ideas about him, even though such knowledge about him was certainly regarded as important. On the other hand much of the origin and development of the literature of the Old Testament can be traced to a historical interest, such as that concerning the occupation of the land of Canaan, or to an interest in the institutions of Israel's religion and the proper order of its worship. As a result even very important and basic ideas about God appear primarily in relation to observances of the cult, as is the case, for example, with the prohibition on the use of images of the deity. This cannot simply be converted by a kind of theological alchemy, into a timeless affirmation of divine incorporeality.

Within British Old Testament scholarship many of the features of the systematic approach to Old Testament theology which appear in the second division of Schultz's work are to be found represented in a volume by A. B. Davidson, which was published posthumously.[8] However the usefulness of this work is seriously impaired by poor editing and the inclusion of material from widely separated periods of Davidson's teaching life. In general, while the aim of presenting an Old Testament theology was not lost sight of by scholars after the achievements of literary criticism in the last quarter of the nineteenth century, a growing conviction began to emerge that such a subject could be better dealt with in the form of a history of Israelite religion. In this way the prevailing historicism threatened to engulf even the more religious and theological aspects of Old Testament study. Several volumes appeared with the aim of presenting such a history of the religion, even though they were almost unanimous in stressing the importance of the emergence of major theological and ethical ideas for the development of Israel's religious life. These histories set such ideas in a context of political events and changing religious institutions. The theological perspective was thereby kept alive by the view of most of such authors that it was precisely on account of its distinctive theological ideas that Israel's religion remained a subject of abiding interest for us. Nonetheless the standpoint was distinctly historical rather than theological.

The effect of this change of attitude is very well exemplified by the study of Old Testament religion by K. Marti.[9] This began initially as a revision of an Old Testament Theology by A. Kayser, but by the third German edition of 1897 Marti had revised it very extensively and changed its title to that of a history of Israelite religion, on the basis of the claim that in this new form the subject could be more adequately dealt with. It is interesting therefore to recognize that confidence in the results of historical criticism had here led to a very substantial shift in methodology in order to interpret the Old Testament theologically. In this regard Marti's work invites comparison with that by Stade, although it is the work of the former scholar which has properly grasped the implications of the method adopted.

At the beginning of the twentieth century considerable changes began to appear in the whole approach to the study of religions, with fresh subjects receiving attention and new methods of enquiry being employed in order to pursue them. These new interests concerned both the rediscovery and evaluation of ancient religions, together with a new concern with the study of contemporary religions. As a result such simple formulae of comparison as those employed by H. Schultz with regard to Israel's religion could no longer be considered seriously as adequate. The wide range of such developments cannot be explored here in detail, but foremost among such new areas of study and methods of enquiry must be placed the growing interest in a phenomenological approach to the study of religion. Not only did this shift the emphasis away from simple evaluations of religions in terms of their fundamental ideas, but it challenged the very basis of what had become an essentially 'ideological' approach to the study of religions in which rites and institutions were treated as secondary to, and sometimes claimed to be derivative from, a number of basic religious concepts. For example the study of rites of sacrifice had tended to be treated as an expression of ideas of atonement, with little real interest in the rites themselves. The impact of these changed interests and attitudes gradually began to affect the study of the Old Testament, especially through the writings of the Dutch scholar G. van der Leeuw.[10] When such changed methods were linked with the results achieved by archaeology in recovering a knowledge of the ancient religions of Babylon, Phoenicia and Egypt a very different picture began to emerge. At first the recovery of legal and mythological material from Babylon appeared disconcerting to many Old Testament scholars, as the sharpness of the Bible—Babel controversy testifies. Soon, however, a more balanced approach became possible, and the help afforded by comparative material from these ancient cultures, came to be regarded as indispensable for a fuller understanding of Israel's religion.

We have already pointed to the important influence exerted by the Danish anthropologist V. Grønbech[11] on S. Mowinckel. Mowinckel's study of the Old Testament psalms pleaded strongly for the recognition that the origins of this literature lie deeply rooted in the ancient Israelite cultus. He thereby challenged many of the assumptions that were at that time current regarding the primitive, and even negative, character of Israel's cult. Not only did Mowinckel reawaken an awareness of the importance of cultus to ancient Israel, but his whole understanding of its character and purpose was strongly opposed to the judgements passed upon it by Wellhausen. Far from being indifferent to personal piety, Mowinckel regarded the cult as a most powerful formative influence upon it.

V. Grønbech's influence upon Old Testament studies was also strongly marked in the work of another Scandinavian scholar, J. Pedersen.[12] Whereas Grønbech's major work was on *The Culture of the Teutons*, Pedersen sought to apply similar methods and insights towards recovering an understanding of the life and thought of ancient Israel. A comparison of the major works of the two scholars quickly demonstrates their relatedness, and shows how different from those of Wellhausen were the assumptions and methods employed by Pedersen towards gaining an understanding of Israel's religion. In a number of features Pedersen's work bears traces of a phenomenological approach,

124

and is strongly marked by an attempt to probe into the thought world and psychology of ancient Israel. Its particular understanding of the psychology of ancient cultures has often been given the label 'dynamistic', because of its understanding of, and belief in, the power attaching to thoughts and words. On this account it has rightly been subjected to considerable criticism. Nevertheless Pedersen's conception of the thought world of ancient Israel, in spite of its being overdrawn in many respects, is sufficient to show that 'the truths and precepts of religion' found in the Old Testament are frequently very unlike our own, and cannot simply be assembled systematically into a theology.

A whole range of features show themselves here which overlap between the fields of anthropology and Old Testament study, and the influence of certain leading figures in the world of anthropological study is noteworthy. Besides the work of V. Grønbech we have already had occasion earlier to note the way in which W. Wundt's researches and theories about ethnic psychology affected Old Testament studies in the area of prophecy, and we should also mention the impact exerted by L. Lévy-Bruhl, whose conception of 'primitive thinking'[13] was also confidently carried over into Old Testament researches and used as a tool of interpretation. In the absence of any continuing concern to explore the areas where Old Testament and anthropological studies overlap the tendency has been evident for brief periods of cross-fertilization to be followed by periods of isolation and indifference. The result has been that interpretations have sometimes been held on to in the Old Testament field which have long since ceased to command support from anthropologists.

Nevertheless the overall impact of newer approaches towards the study of the history of religions generally, combined with the insights gained by anthropological researches into both ancient and modern societies, has led to a considerable change of attitude towards the study of the Old Testament, and in particular of Old Testament theology. The result has been a growing awareness that the religious ideas of ancient Israel cannot be studied very easily or fruitfully in isolation from the context of religious and social life in which they functioned. To what extent such ideas can be isolated and systematized at all remains open to further investigation. Nevertheless it is clear that evaluation of the claim to divine revelation in the Old Testament cannot simply be upheld by a hypothesis about the disclosure, or discovery, by Israel of a number of basic religious and ethical ideas. In this connection it appears that the nature of the material preserved in the Old Testament, and the tools of

125

scholarship available to interpret it, have undoubtedly been more favourable to those who have endeavoured to write a historical description of the religion of ancient Israel than to those who have sought to construct an Old Testament theology. Certainly the new insights of critical scholarship of the late nineteenth century were most suited to recovering a fresh picture of the history of Israelite religion.

The continued awareness of the difficulty of presenting an Old Testament theology which could be distinguished both in its purpose and method from an account of the history of Israelite-Jewish religion has carried us far beyond the time when Schultz's work was first published. His twofold division into historical and systematic treatments appeared a convenient way of handling the material, even though both divisions assumed that the task was primarily a descriptive one. The multitude of apologetic and evaluative judgements contained in the work are presented as though they were embedded in the Old Testament material itself. Nonetheless it is very evident that Schultz was a Christian theologian who felt that the proper sequel to the Old Testament revelation was to be found in the Christian faith. Whereas earlier nineteenth century Protestant scholars like E. W. von Hengstenberg, with his *Christology of the Old Testament*,[14] and J. C. K. von Hofmann,[15] with his conception of Old Testament promise and New Testament fulfilment, had endeavoured to relate the two testaments by theological schemes, H. Schultz was claiming to present his theology within the limits imposed by critical historical research. The question could rightly be raised whether this was not in fact forcing the method of historical criticism to yield results which were more theological than historical. In the event the marked degree to which theological considerations have influenced Schultz's conclusions is undeniable, and this can certainly be seen to be the case in the work of other scholars as well.

The marriage between theology and history has not run smoothly, and not for the first time the question of the presuppositions which have influenced various scholars' interpretations has had to be raised. In 1925 C. Steuernagel published a short essay in which he raised afresh the question of the difference of method required by an Old Testament theology, over against a history of Israelite religion.[16] Shortly afterwards O. Eissfeldt argued in favour of a separation between the historical-critical approach to the study of Israel's religion and the theological evaluation required for an Old Testament theology.[17] This latter would then be quite free to fasten upon those aspects which the author of such a theology himself favoured on the basis of his own religious standpoint. Thus, whilst the critical historian would set himself the task of describing what he found in the Old Testament as impartially as possible, the theologian would readily reveal his partiality by the value judgements which he upheld. Eissfeldt's own work shows his personal concern to pursue the task of the impartial historian. Even so his short essay serves to adumbrate a deep-seated problem in the task of writing an Old Testament theology which has continued to be keenly felt by other scholars.

As a result the question of whether the subject should be, or even can be, dealt with in a purely descriptive way has frequently been prefaced to treatments of it. The majority of scholars have tended to decide in favour of pursuing a descriptive aim since this can most readily claim to conform to the canons of critical historical method. Thus Old Testament theologians have generally set themselves the task of describing the theological ideas contained in the Old Testament. Scholars who have attempted this, however, have usually been criticized on the grounds that it is usually not difficult to tell the author's own confessional attachment to a particular religious standpoint and too often the tenets and interests of western European Protestant Christianity have readily been discernible in much that has been written on the subject of Old Testament theology.

Standing rather alone among major writers on Old Testament theology Th.C. Vriezen has argued that the proper starting point for a theology of the Old Testament is to be found in an awareness that the true goal of the Old Testament lies in the New Testament.[18] However when it comes to a detailed study of Vriezen's presentation of the material it is hard to see how this overt Christian starting point has been incorporated into the material. Even more explicit was the earlier attempt of W. Vischer to revive a form of typological exegesis as a means of affirming the Christian theological meaning of the Old Testament.[19] Here the whole proceeding has become so arbitrary and detached from the historico-critical approach to the meaning of the Old Testament that it has understandably failed to receive any significant following.

The dangers of falling into an uncontrolled, and historically unsound, interpretation are evident enough, so that it is easy to see why to most scholars it has appeared sounder to work within the framework of a historical and descriptive approach. Yet even here theological evaluations have tended to make a surprising, and sometimes prominent, appearance. In particular questions concerning the genuineness of experiences of God and of the truth of prophetic revelations have readily entered into the discussions, even though they properly fall outside the framework of a rigidly historical and descriptive approach. On the other side it may be argued that it belongs to the very nature of theology to be evaluative and to pass judgements which lie outside a purely historical framework. Thus it is hard to see that a satisfactory Old Testament theology can be written which concerns itself solely with stating what Israel believed, and which does not go on to question and discuss more widely the truth of Israel's religious ideas. In spite of the uncritical and historically unacceptable methods of exegesis present in the works of such nineteenth century scholars as E. W. von Hengstenberg and J. C. K. von Hofmann, we can nevertheless recognize the theological interest and purpose of their work. There is therefore an issue of very central significance in Eissfeldt's attempt at a distinction of method between an Old Testament theology and a history of Israelite religion. Whilst he himself was most immediately concerned to establish a truly disciplined and critical approach to the history of religion, and to leave the theologian at the mercy of a certain arbitrariness of judgement, this is not the inevitable consequence of his distinction.

Within Old Testament studies the question whether there is room for an independent discipline of Old Testament theology alongside the historical study of Israel's religion was raised again in 1929 by W. Eichrodt.[20] Recognizing the unsatisfactoriness of the twofold division used by H. Schultz, Eichrodt sought some way of obviating such an awkward separation. How could Old Testament faith be looked at honestly both in its dimension of historical depth, which spanned approximately a thousand years, and also systematically in a natural correlation of its religious ideas? What was needed was some principle of order and unity which would allow the great variety of religious ideas to be looked at in a systematic way and grouped together. This principle of unity Eichrodt found in the concept of the covenant between God and Israel. Hence when he came to present his extensive two-volume *Theology of the Old Testament*[21] the great multiplicity of ideas attested in the Old Testament regarding God, man and the world were interrelated by this concept. In many respects Eichrodt's use of the idea of covenant as a principle of unity marked a major step forward so that even though it has called forth much criticism and discussion it must be recognized as having drawn attention to a fundamental problem relating to the basic task of interpreting the Old Testament as theology. What is the principle of unity by which the religious ideas of the Old Testament can be related to each other so as to provide some recognizable basis for a systematic theology?

In some respects Eichrodt's fastening upon the concept of covenant only partially fulfilled his purpose since the Hebrew word *berith* (covenant) itself is used very unevenly throughout the Old Testament. In some areas, especially the book of Deuteronomy and other writings influenced extensively by it (the history from Joshua to 2 Kings and the book of Jeremiah) it appears very frequently, whereas in the older literature it is rarely used and in other parts of the Old Testament also it is very much in the background (the Psalms, the Wisdom writings). Nevertheless Eichrodt was concerned not with the study of the word as such, but with the conscious awareness expressed in the Old Testament of a relationship existing between God and Israel which was capable of being described in more than one way, and for which the term 'covenant' served as one very basic concept. In more recent treatments of the problem scholars have endeavoured to widen the formal scope of Eichrodt's insight whilst retaining its essential character by seeking to present the unity of the Old Testament in the ideas pointing to the relationship between God and Israel.

Undoubtedly if the awkward twofold division initiated by Schultz is to be avoided some unifying principle becomes necessary of the kind advocated by Eichrodt, unless we are to be left with a mere miscellaneous and disconnected collection of religious ideas. Several scholars have looked elsewhere for such a principle, usually in the idea of God, or in some understanding of his activity, such as his sovereignty or his communion with man. The danger of such alternatives has been that they easily become too broad, and thereby fail to explain the more distinctive characteristics of the Old Testament literature. As a result they could quite easily be made to apply to a vastly wider religious literature than that contained in the Old Testament. Thus they hardly reach to its core.

Eichrodt could rightly contend that the relationship between God and Israel was consciously and undeniably a central point of interest for the Old Testament literature. Through the varied forms which Israel took during the Old Testament period of its history, such as tribal federation, territorial state and religious community, and the various ways in which God was conceived and worshipped throughout the long time-span covered, their mutual relationship was nonetheless continually assumed. Yahweh is the God of Israel and Israel is the people of Yahweh. In consequence the reader finds that whereas the religious ideas concerning the nature of God, man and salvation appear uppermost in the traditional divisions of systematic theology they appear in the Old Testament only secondarily to ideas of the divine election of Israel, its covenant relationship to God and its divinely appointed role to be a witness to the nations. While a theology of the Old Testament cannot close its eyes to the former, it must come to them through the ideas which the Old Testament itself employs in regard to the relationship between God and Israel. From his position Eichrodt can justifiably claim to be working within the range of religious concepts which have given rise to the Old Testament literature which we possess, rather than to be intruding a system of theological order upon the Old Testament which is alien to its essential character. This endeavour to uncover the essential character and themes of the Old Testament, rather than to reconstruct an ancient Israelite theology as a kind of prefigurement of modern Christian systematic theology, accounts for many of the marked differences which characterize volumes dealing with the subject. In consequence it is inevitable that a good deal of uncertainty and variety marks the various treatments which have followed Eichrodt's work, resulting from the different arrangements adopted for the ordering of the Old Testament material.

Eichrodt's achievement has been a remarkable one. It has undoubtedly established a place for Old Testament theology with a status and method of its own as an independent subject within Old Testament and theological studies. Yet it has also called forth much criticism, sufficient to raise the question whether an undertaking of this nature is really possible along the lines advocated, in view of the nature of the Old Testament literature. Within Eichrodt's work the reader can discern much of the legacy of nineteenth century idealism which found no difficulty in setting ideas apart, and looking at them in isolation, as the real jewels of human achievement. Although Eichrodt rightly sought to work within the ideas actually found in the Old Testament, it may be objected that he has abstracted them, and removed them from their context in history and life, in such a way as to misrepresent their original importance to Israel. They are like pictures ripped from their frames and stored in a heap. Thus the impression is left upon the reader that the enduring contribution of Israel's cultus was simply to have served as a vehicle for symbolizing and communicating religious ideas and instruction.

Furthermore the very quest for a unifying principle tends too easily to mask the disunity and tensions within the Old Testament. Eichrodt's cross-section of faith in the Old Testament is very much an artificial reconstruction because no one figure of ancient Israel can be shown to have consciously held such a system of beliefs. It is produced out of the amalgam of faiths of many different figures of considerably different ages. In particular the great differences between the early religion of Israel prior to the downfall of the monarchy, with its central focus on cultic activity, and the subsequent early Jewish faith of the post-exilic age in which already a written law was achieving canonical authority are most marked. The gradual transition from a religion of a cultus to a religion of a book lies at the heart of the formation and authority of the Old Testament as a sacred literature. It is right therefore to be critical of any presentation of an Old Testament theology which fails to show clearly the movements which led to the production of a canon of Old Testament scripture. J. Wellhausen had contrasted very sharply the high point of prophetic faith in the pre-exilic and exilic ages with the *torah*-centered biblicism of later Judaism of which he was intensely critical. Even admitting a considerable degree of over-emphasis in Wellhausen's position, it must be argued that Eichrodt has obscured the marked differences of outlook between the two periods.

On the question of the understanding of covenant itself, Eichrodt's theology has undoubtedly contributed towards a strengthened desire to investigate the history and significance of such a concept in the Old Testament. Here two very distinct lines of interpretation have developed. The first of these has followed up the researches of G. E. Mendenhall in which he has argued that the tradition of the Sinai covenant, as portrayed in the Decalogue of Exodus 20: 2–17, reveals Israel's adoption of the form of ancient Near Eastern vassal-treaties.[22] He interpreted this as a consequence of the fact that Moses would have been familiar with the form of such political treaties in Egypt, and must have adopted this for the specific religious and political needs of the emergent people of Israel. These were to be the vassal people of Yahweh, their sovereign deity, who protected them against all forms of moral, religious, and political slavery. Under such a divine soveriegn, no human figure was to be allowed to usurp his position of ultimate authority. A considerable company of scholars has followed along the path marked out by Mendenhall, often extending it into bypaths which Mendenhall himself has been unwilling to tread.[23] Even so the hypothesis in general has aroused intense interest in the form and background of covenants and covenant-ceremonies in the Old Testament which has served to clarify the evidence which is to be found there, and to set it in the light of a much wider background. On the debit side the hypothesis has sometimes ignored the proper canons of form criticism, and has stressed the significance of similarities between various accounts of treaties and covenants while ignoring equally important differences and dissimilarities.

In another direction a revived interest in the Old Testament use of the term 'covenant' and the range of concepts which it connotes, has led to an extensive lexicographical and semantic study of the Hebrew word *berith* (usually translated 'covenant'). Here mention needs to be made of the work of scholars such as G. Quell, J. Begrich, and A. Jepsen.[24] However, it is most especially in the work of E. Kutsch that the semantic task has been carried through with great vigour, to establish by actual contextual examinations the various ways in which *berith* was understood in ancient Israel.[25] Kutsch shows how the idea of imposing an obligation led on to an interpretation of covenant, on the one hand as law and on the other as 'promise.' Working to some degree with the same material, L. Perlitt has endeavoured to clarify the theological meaning and significance of covenant in the Old Testament.[26] In particular, he has sharply attacked the form-critical studies of Mendenhall and has argued that the theology of covenant must be tied inseparably to the actual usage of the term *berith*. This has resulted in his returning in a number of prominent respects to views about the rise of a theology of covenant in ancient Israel similar to those of J. Wellhausen. Notably, this includes an awareness that a certain legalistic element is potentially present in the description of Israel's relationship to God as a covenant, a view which is not substantiated by Kutsch's studies.

While this research into the meaning of covenant in the Old Testament has provided a welcome adjunct to Eichrodt's theological position, in reality the latter has been less markedly affected by it than may at first sight appear. This is because Eichrodt's introduction of the term 'covenant' as a key unifying factor in the Old Testament has been less concerned with the word and its semantic history and more with the reality it connotes, which is the relationship between Yahweh and Israel. It is not without interest, however, that over against Perlitt, Eichrodt has risen in defence of the claim that the term *berith* was used quite early in Israel to describe this relationship.[27]

Eichrodt's approach to the subject of Old Testament theology started from the assumption that the material proper to such a subject must be the religious ideas current in ancient Israel about God and his relationship to man, both Israelite man in particular and ultimately all mankind, including the universe in which man's life is spent. In spite of many marked differences of detail this view of the task of the Old Testament theologian shares many features in common with the nineteenth century historians of Israel's religion who argued that the primary contribution of this religion to mankind has been its affirmation of a doctrine of ethical monotheism. Clearly this is a broad position from which no serious Old Testament scholar would wish to dissent, yet it is also firmly evident that Israel did not itself isolate and systematize its religious doctrines in this fashion. Such a precisely formulated concept as 'ethical monotheism' is not found in the Old Testament, and its very abstractness is somewhat alien to its thought forms. Usually in the Old Testament the main religious ideas appear in relation to the political, cultic and social life of the nation. Furthermore, when we enquire about the way in which the literature of the Old Testament expresses these ideas, we find that it very frequently does so by recounting the history of Israel and its institutions. Its writings were not written to provide summaries, or compendia, of religious ideas, but as records of events, prophecies and religious practices of this people. Hence one of the most significant limitations of Eichrodt's presentation of an Old Testament theology is that it offers too little by way of explanation of how Judaism became a religion of a book. Nor is it made clear how the Old Testament literature serves to communicate the fundamental religious ideas revealed to ancient Israel.

Undoubtedly Eichrodt's volumes must rank in the forefront of the endeavour to re-establish Old Testament theology as a viable theological discipline after its decline at the end of the nineteenth century. Several other volumes appeared in its support, with various differences of emphasis, but with substantially the same basic assumptions about the way in which the subject should be tackled. Among these we may list the volumes by L. Köhler, Th.C. Vriezen and E. Jacob.[28] New questionings began to arise, however, about the nature of such a theological enterprise, asking whether what was being achieved could be regarded as an adequate theological interpretation of the Old Testament literature. Certainly no one could doubt that such theologies had strayed some way from the main interests of a critical historical exegesis of its writings. In recognition of this A. Weiser argued that the theological task must lie with exegesis itself, and with the exposition of the message of the word of God as it is contained in the Old Testament writings.[29] The outcome of this assertion has been the appearance of a series of commentaries on the Old Testament (*Das Alte Testament Deutsch*) which has endeavoured to re-establish a place for theological comment and exposition within a truly critical and literary-historical framework of exegesis.[30] Several volumes in the series have been exceptionally fruitful and well-received, but have not even so shown any one consistent pattern of theological interpretation.

A very different approach to the problem of writing an Old Testament theology appeared with the work of G. von Rad.[31] In this a variety of influences can be seen to have been at work, but before we enquire into them it is useful to look at the way in which von Rad has set about his task. This begins with a recognition that a theology of the Old Testament must properly recognize that it is this literature itself which forms its essential subject matter, and not simply the religious ideas which were current in ancient Israel. In fact it is a striking feature of ancient Israelite religion that it did not deliberately abstract its theological ideas and form them into a coherent and self-contained body of doctrine. Nor did it formulate a creed as a rounded summary of basic ideas about God and his relationship to the world. Rather the creed of ancient Israel was a short summary of the great acts of God by which he had chosen this people to be his and had bound them to himself. This short 'credo', or kerygma, was found most clearly expressed by von Rad in certain Old Testament passages, most especially Deut. 6: 20–24; 26: 5b–9 and Joshua 24: 2b–13. By this kerygma Israel confessed who Yahweh was, and how as a people they had become related to him. This divine election had especially brought to Israel God's gifts, most notably the gift of the land of Canaan.

Von Rad argued that, although these short summaries were now preserved in relatively late texts (7th century or later), they were of much earlier origin. They witnessed to the brief confessional recital of Yahweh's saving will towards his people which had once formed the central fact in Israel's distinctive tradition of worship. Thus they recounted a *Heilsgeschichte*, a history of salvation (the term goes back to the nineteenth century Erlangen scholar, J. C. K. von Hofmann). Such a recital of the *Heilsgeschichte* provided Israel with its basic knowledge of God. We have already had occasion to note in the study of the interpretation of the Pentateuch that von Rad had used this insight to provide a means of unravelling the structure and origin of the J documentary source. In his theology, however, von Rad's arguments ranged beyond showing how the early cultus of Israel had used such credal summaries to provide the people with a knowledge of who yahweh was and why they should worship him. It was a light by which the entire extent of the Pentateuch which we now have could be illuminated. Fundamentally this is a historical literature, and its record of past events is a witness to the existence and will of Yahweh, as this had been made known to his people by his actions.

When we proceed to examine the theology of the prophetic literature, which several scholars had accorded the primary place in Israel's theological development, von Rad argued that this must be seen in the light of the older election-traditions to which the Pentateuch witnessed. For this reason the place and status of the prophets in the Hebrew canon as coming after the Law (the Pentateuch) was recognized as theologically correct. The most abiding feature of Israelite prophecy was the way in which it had viewed the history and faith of Israel at a crucial period in the nation's existence, and had interpreted this in the light of the law. The prophets had thereby invested the law with a new, and more radical, significance. In consequence prophecy represented a kind of renewal, or resumption, of the older kerygmatic *Heilsgeschichte*, but now viewing it in a reverse way as a history of God's judgement upon his people. The decline in the nation's fortunes which took place in the eighth to sixth centuries was thereby seen as included within God's saving purpose, but regarded as a necessary expression of the divine wrath against Israel's disobedience. By looking beyond these acts of judgement to further acts of re-election and renewal for Israel in the future, the prophets carried the history of salvation beyond the present. In the process they established a kind of typology by which the future work of divine re-election was portrayed in terms of the older election-traditions. At the same time this prophetic promise for the future lent to the Old Testament as a whole a distinct openness, in which the history of salvation was seen as a process which was still awaiting completion and fulfilment.

All in all therefore, von Rad argued that the prophetic parts of the Old Testament in no way stand apart from the older historical traditions preserved in the Pentateuch. On the contrary they are familiar with, and make use of, these traditions, projecting them forward into the future to affirm a coming act of divine completion of the history of salvation. This fulfilment was readily seen by the early Christian church to have been achieved in the life and work of Jesus of Nazareth. Admittedly, von Rad recognized that some features of the Old Testament could not too easily be accommodated in this scheme which started from the accounts of Israel's election-traditions as a *Heilsgeschichte*. Most notably this was true of the Psalms and the wisdom writings, which von Rad placed by themselves at the end of the first volume of his theology as witnessing to

Israel's response to God's saving actions.

Undoubtedly, when viewed as a whole, this fresh presentation of the nature and method of Old Testament theology has had a most profound impact upon the theological world. It has stimulated a vast range of secondary literature to deal with issues it has raised, and has compelled the most extensive re-examination of the very possibility of an Old Testament theology and the methods it must employ. After its completion von Rad himself devoted his energies to a much more extensive investigation of the problems of the theological place and significance of Israel's wisdom tradition.[32] His death took place suddenly in 1971, after a brief illness.

Before considering the merits of this fresh evaluation of the character and method of Old Testament theology, we may look briefly at some of its antecedents. For the way in which von Rad related his theology to the form and composition of the Old Testament literature, especially that of the Pentateuch, we can readily recognize the strong influence of Hermann Gunkel. The form-critical and traditio-historical insights initiated by Gunkel's study of Genesis are extended much further by von Rad into the whole area of the Pentateuch. By this means the study of the literary growth of the Pentateuch is linked very effectively with the theological conception of a *Heilsgeschichte*. Hence a category of theological thought and interpretation, which had already acquired a special significance in biblical, especially New Testament, studies is used to illuminate the whole structure of the Old Testament and its theology. This literature did not contain one uniform theology, or set of theological ideas, but a whole sequence of such theologies. These did not take the form of a compact creed, but rather, were a recounting of history in which succeeding generations of Israelites affirmed and interpreted faith in their own divine election. Thus, instead of the historical dimension proving an awkward complication, as Eichrodt and others before him had found in seeking a historical cross-section of faith, it was of the very essence of the Old Testament literature and its theology. History-writing provided the ancient Israelites with their primary mode of theological affirmation and expression. On the positive side, therefore, von Rad had been very successful in writing a theology which took seriously the nature of the Old Testament literature and its subject matter.

On the negative side two points in particular may be raised in criticism of von Rad's work. The first of these is that by so emphasizing the diversity of theological thought in the Old Testament, he has done less than justice to equally valid and significant aspects of its inter-connections and unifying elements. As a result it stops short of bringing the various expressions of faith together in a way which is sufficiently systematic and co-ordinated to establish a satisfactory basis of theological evaluation. The second point of criticism is related to this, and serves in part to explain the reason for it. It is that the traditio-historical method is used so extensively as a key to understanding the structure of the Old Testament literature, that the method itself tends to dominate the kind of results which it produces. Particularly is this so in regard to the prophets, where the impact upon each of them of specific election-traditions which they presuppose becomes so over-ridingly evi-dent in their interpretation as to crowd out other, equally important, factors relating to contemporary life and events. This is not only true of the prophets, however, but also affects other parts of the literature, where, for example only slight attention is paid to the Pentateuch in its final form, or even in the latter stages of its redaction. To this extent the formation of the J, E and P documents as independent compositions is still regarded as more meaningful than their combination and redaction into a larger whole—yet it is these latter stages of growth which characterize most deeply the Old Testament which we have.

All in all, however, it would be an error not to recognize the great originality and freshness which has marked von Rad's approach to Old Testament theology. He has certainly done much to point out the limitations of the more traditional systematic approaches, which fail to capture the essential nature of the Old Testament. In many ways they foster the image of an abstract and static theology which is quite unlike the rich and varied historical nature of the literature which it seeks to interpret.

Since von Rad completed his Old Testament theology several further works bearing this title have appeared, in addition to the many studies which have been devoted to examining further what such a subject should be, and what are its outstanding problems. The volume by G. Fohrer[33] provides a significant complement to his earlier book on the history of Israelite religion. Its particular concern has been to uncover the distinctive intellectual world of the Old Testament, and to show how the major foundations of Christian theology are already laid in its writings, with a separation of religion from magic and mythology, and the establishing of a truly personal and theistic conception of God. Hence Fohrer does much to illuminate the world-view of the ancient Israelite, and the importance of this for religion, without especially relating this to the structure of the Old Testament literature as von Rad has done. To this extent Fohrer's work is a valuable guide to an understanding of how ancient Israelite man thought. At the same time it poses many problems, since it is evident that these religious ideas belonged to a cultic and cultural milieu which is no longer with us. What is needed is a clearer demonstration of how the Old Testament forms a bridge between our own theological needs and the very different needs of ancient Israel.

In a short study which is promised as a preparation for a larger work, W. Zimmerli has endeavoured to carry the task of writing an Old Testament theology a stage further.[35] Already earlier, in critiques of von Rad's work, Zimmerli had expressed his deep appreciation of this scholar's approach, but had indicated that he felt that it had stressed too heavily the elements of diversity in the Old Testament.[36] It is not surprising therefore that in his work he has sought to do fuller justice to the more unifying features which hold together the Old Testament. Perhaps most of all the influence of von Rad is to be seen in the way in which Zimmerli has drawn attention to those particular themes which loom so prominently in the Old Testament writings: the gifts of God in land, priesthood and kingship.

Overall there is no doubt that the search for a satisfactory way of presenting the theological message of the Old Testament remains unfinished. While something of a pause has been in order, to enable scholars to digest adequately the work that has been done in the past thirty years, and especially to take in fully von Rad's criticisms of much of this, it is evident that several more volumes on the subject may be expected in the coming decades. Increasingly it has become plain that issues which seemed at one time capable of being dealt with as prolegomena belong to the very centre of the theological interpretation of the Old Testament. Questions regarding its basic unity, its relationship to the New Testament and to Judaism, and its relevance to the modern world, are not matters for cursory treatment in a preface, but belong to the heart of what an Old Testament theology should be.

---

1. J. Wellhausen, 'Israel', *Prolegomena to the History of Israel*, p. 47.
2. J. Wellhausen, *ibid.*, p. 474.
3. B. Stade, *Biblische Theologie des Alten Testaments*, Bd. I, Tübingen, 1905: Bd. II by A. Bertholet was published in 1911.
4. G. Schultz, *Alttestamentliche Theologie*, Braunschweig, 1869–89, English

translation by J. A. Paterson, *Old Testament Theology*, 2 Volumes, Edinburgh, 1892.

5. H. Schultz, *Old Testament Theology*, Volume I, p. 52.

6. E. Sellin, *Alttestamentliche Theologie auf religionsgeschichtlicher Grundlage; Erster Teil: Israelitisch-jüdische Religionsgeschichte; Zweiter Teil: Theologie des Alten Testaments*, Leipzig, 1933.

7. O. Procksch, *Theologie des Alten Testaments*, Gutersloh, 1950.

8. A. B. Davidson, *Old Testament Theology*, edited by S. D. F. Salmond, Edinburgh, 1904.

9. K. Marti, *Geschichte der Israelitischen Religion, 4. Verbesserte Auflage von August Kayser's Theologie des Alten Testaments*, Strassburg, 1903.

10. G. van der Leeuw, *Phänomenologie der Religion*, Göttingen, 1933. English translation by J. E. Turner, *Religion in Essence and Manifestation*, London, 1938.

11. V. Grønbech, *The Culture of the Teutons*, translated by W. Worster, London-Copenhagen, 1931. A new edition of the original Danish *Vor Folkaet i Oldtiden*, was published in 1955 (Copenhagen, 2 volumes in 1).

12. J. Pedersen, *Israel. Its Life and Culture*, I–II, Copenhagen, 1926; III–IV, 1940.

13. Especially in L. Lévy-Bruhl, *La mentalité primitive*, Paris, 1922. English translation by L. A. Clare, *Primitive Mentality*, London, 1923.

14. Von Hengstenberg, *The Christology of the Old Testament*, translated by T. Meyer, 4 volumes, Edinburgh, 1854–8. The original German *Christologie des Alten Testaments* was published in 3 volumes in Berlin in 1829–35. A reprint of the English translation by R. Keith with some abridgement by T. K. Arnold was published in 1956 (Grand Rapids, Michigan).

15. J. C. K. von Hofmann, *Weissagung und Erfüllung im Alten und Neuen Testament*, 1841–55.

16. C. Steuernagel, 'Alttestamentliche Theologie und Alttestamentliche Religionsgeschichte', *Vom Alten Testament. K. Marti Festschrift*, edited by K. Budde (*BZAW* 41), Giessen, 1925.

17. O. Eissfeldt, 'Israelitisch-jüdische Religionsgeschichte und alttestamentliche Theologie', in *ZAW* 44 (1926), pp. 1–12.

18. Th. C. Vriezen, *Hoofdlijnen der Theologie van het Oude Testament*, Wageningen, 1949; English translation, *An Outline of Old Testament Theology*, Oxford, 1958; revised edition 1968. A survey and critique on Vriezen's approach by me is to be found in *Contemporary Old Testament Theologians*, edited by R. B. Laurin, Valley Forge, 1970, pp. 121–140.

19. W. Vischer, *Das Christuszeugnis des Alten Testaments*, Bd. I, Zürich, 1934; Bd. II, Zürich, 1942. English translation of volume I *The Witness of the Old Testament to Christ*, by A. B. Crabtree.

20. W. Eichrodt, 'Hat die alttestamentliche Theologie noch selbständige Bedeutung innerhalb der alttestamentliche Wissenschaft?', in *ZAW* 47 (1929), pp. 83–91.

21. W. Eichrodt, *Theologie des Alten Testaments*, Bd. I, Stuttgart, 1933; Bd. II, 1935; Bd. III, 1939; English translation by J. A. Baker, *Theology of the Old Testament*, Volume I, London, 1969; Volume II, 1967.

22. See above p. 22 and see now his book *The Tenth Generation. The Origins of the Biblical Tradition*, Baltimore, 1973.
23. For these developments cf. the survey volume by D. J. McCarthy, *Covenant in the Old Testament. A Survey of Current Opinions*, Oxford, 1972.
24. G. Quell, article in *Theologisches Wörterbuch zum Neuen Testament*, Bd. II, 1935, pp. 106–127. English translation by G. W. Bromiley, *Theological Dictionary of the New Testament*, Volume II, Grand Rapids, 1964, pp. 106–121.

    J. Begrich, 'Berit. Ein Beitrag zur Erfassung einer alttestamentliche Denkform', in *ZAW* 60 (1944), pp. 1–11 (=*Geschichte Studien zum Alten Testament*, edited by W. Zimmerli, Munich, 1964, pp. 55–66.

    A. Jepsen, 'Berith. Ein Beitrag zur Theologie der Exilszeit', *Verbannung und Heimkehr. W. Rudolph Festschrift*, Tübingen, 1961, pp. 161–180.
25. E. Kutsch, *Verheissung und Gesetz* (*BZAW* 131), Berlin and New York, 1973. Cf. also his essay 'Gottes Zuspruch und Anspruch. *berit* in der alttestamentlichen Theologie', *Questions disputées d'Ancien Testament. Méthode et Théologie* (Bibl. Ephem. Theol. Lovan. xxxiii, 1974), pp. 71–90.
26. L. Perlitt, *Bundestheologie des Alten Testaments* (*WMANT* 36), Neukirchen-Vluyn, 1969.
27. W. Eichrodt, 'Darf man heute noch von einem Gottesbund mit Israel reden?', in *Th.Z.* 30 (1974), pp. 193–206.
28. L. Köhler, *Theologie des Alten Testaments*, Stuttgart, 1935; English translation by A. S. Todd, *Old Testament Theology*, London, 1958.

    E. Jacob, *Théologie de l'Ancien Testament*, 1955; deuxième édition, 1968. English translation of the first edition by A. W. Heathcote and P. J. Allcock, *Theology of the Old Testament*, London, 1958.

    For the volume by Vriezen see above note 18.
29. A. Weiser, 'Die theologische Aufgabe der alttestamentlichen Wissenschaft', in *Glaube und Geschichte im Alten Testament*, Göttingen, 1966, pp. 182–200. The original essay was published in Stuttgart in 1935.
30. Several of these volumes have been translated into English and published in the series Old Testament Library by SCM and Westminster Presses.
31. G. von Rad, *Theologie des Alten Testaments*, Bd. I, Munich, 1957; Bd. II, 1962, English translation by D. M. G. Stalker, *Theology of the Old Testament*, Edinburgh and London, Volume I, 1962; Volume II, 1965.
32. G. von Rad, *Weisheit in Israel*, Munich, 1970; English translation by J. D. Martin, *Wisdom in Israel*, London, 1972.
33. G. Fohrer, *Theologische Grundstrukturen des Alten Testaments*, Berlin and New York, 1972.
34. G. Fohrer, *Geschichte der Israelitischen Religion*, Berlin, 1969; English translation by D. Green, *A History of Israelite Religion*, London, 1973.
35. W. Zimmerli, *Grundriss der alttestamentlichen Theologie*, Stuttgart, Berlin, Cologne and Mainz, 1972.
36. See his essay 'Alttestamentliche Traditionsgeschichte und Theologie' in *Probleme biblischer Theologie* edited by H. W. Wolff, Munich, 1971, pp. 632–647.

8

Retrospect and Prospect

In surveying the achievements of a century of intense and devoted critical scholarship centred on the Old Testament a number of features stand out. Perhaps foremost among these is a sense of necessity, and even of inevitability, that such a scholarly and religious enterprise should have been embarked upon. Although our brief sketch began with the work of Wellhausen, it would be wrong to regard him as the initiator of a new critical approach to the Old Testament. Rather, as he himself fully recognized, all the tools of critical method were already to hand when he began, and the major individual pieces of his critical reappraisal had already taken shape in the hands of earlier scholars. What he did was to fit them together in a way that was at once both simple, practicable and generally convincing.

Nor indeed should we suppose that it was simply the availability of effective critical tools that gave rise to the new perspective in biblical studies, for behind them lay a much deeper philosophical, spiritual and cultural concern with human history, especially the history of man's religious and spiritual development. Indeed it was this deep concern with the springs of man's spiritual history that had led to the fashioning of the appropriate scholarly tools and methods. The historical concern of the German Romantic movement, focused especially in the writings of J. G. Herder (1744–1803), had already pointed directly to the literature of the Old Testament as a vital fountainhead of spiritual enlightenment and it is generally recognized that this exercised a wide influence over the religious and literary outlook of nineteenth century Germany, fostering a fresh historical concern with the Old Testament literature. So too did the philosophy of G. W. F. Hegel (1770–1831), with its special interest in man's spiritual history. From a very different direction the religious pietism, which so deeply affected German life and religion in the eighteenth and nineteenth centuries, fed impulses of its own into the minds of men searching for a clearer understanding of their religious past. G. Ebeling has shown[1] that it was this pietism which engendered the search for a biblical theology to serve as a guide and critique for the more systematic endeavours of the dogmaticians, and to feed the faith of the devout Christian. The series of attempts to produce such a biblical theology in the nineteenth century, especially in the hands of German scholars, some of whom such as W. Vatke (1806–1882) were quite radical in their approach, fostered the need for some better historical perspective by which to control the Old Testament literature than that provided by the traditional account of its origins. It is of relevant interest therefore to find that several of the leading scholars of the period, such as Wellhausen and Gunkel in Germany and Robertson Smith in Scotland, were sons of practising ministers of the Christian church.

A further influence has also been suggested as significant for an understanding of Wellhausen's work, and this is to be found in the new German political consciousness that was flourishing in the latter half of the nineteenth century. The age of Bismarck and the growth of German unity were factors which affected very profoundly the life and thought of German universities at this time. Hence it does not cause surprise to find echoes of this in the work of German historians in their researches into more remote ages. In many ways this is well exemplified in the person of Heinrich Ewald, the revered teacher of both Wellhausen and Duhm, who was very powerfully active in political life.[2] More subtly it has been regarded as evident in the way in which Wellhausen assessed the importance of ancient Israel's national consciousness.[3] That Israel as a nation was a more robust and attractive entity than Israel as a dispersed community, or 'Church', is a judgement which is readily apparent in Wellhausen's presentation of Israel's history. So too is his interest in Israel's 'national will' and 'national spirit'.

Along with this concern it is appropriate to consider the attitude of the new critical scholarship to Judaism. At several points it is clear from the repeated interest that he displayed in the subject that the rise of Pharisaism and the development of Judaism as a religion of law were regarded by Wellhausen as a sharp decline from the higher achievements of pre-exilic Israelite religion. The loss of Israel's national consciousness, and the attempt to confine spiritual and moral insights into a code of laws were seen as contradicting the great truths of man's freedom and responsibility which had been proclaimed by the prophets. Wellhausen's interest in his own German culture in the Romantic tradition of Herder is no doubt also a relevant fact regarding his rather negative assessment of Judaism as a religion of people who had lost their national consciousness and unity. A more extreme representative of such a pro-German viewpoint is to be found in the person of Paul de Lagarde, who was Wellhausen's immediate predecessor in the chair of Semitic Languages at Göttingen, and an ardent supporter of German national unity.

Without entering into a separate discussion of the validity of such judgements, it is sufficient here to notice that this viewpoint, which was taken up by others, did tend to create an image of the critical study of the Old Testament as being somewhat anti-Jewish in tendency. Very regrettably it was capable of being distorted in this direction by some scholars and theologians in the years of Nazi dominance in Germany. Yet such was certainly not intentionally the case with the majority of scholars, and it must be noted that many stood out very courageously in opposition to the prevalent wave of anti-Semitic feeling in Germany precisely because of their allegiance to the Old Testament. There can therefore be no overall validity to the claim that the new critical methods of study of the Old Testament were motivated by anti-Semitic feeling or concern. Increasingly over the years the growing participation of Jewish scholars in the critical interpretation of the Old Testament, and in seeking to promote its disciplines, has increased in strength and fruitfulness. One of the great attractions that this more critical historical approach has possessed for scholars has been the expectation that it can provide a common meeting place between Jews and Christians by moving beyond the traditional lines of their respective modes of apologetic.

Once the goal of a critical historical approach to the literature of the Old Testament has been embraced it becomes a leaven which transforms everything.[4] No part of the literature can be left unexamined, and everything becomes subject to review. That this has resulted in the emergence of a picture of the origins of the literature, and the course of Israelite-Jewish history in which it was produced, which differs greatly from that which had previously been upheld by Jewish and Christian tradition is incontrovertible. It was inevitable that this should have proved disconcerting to the faith of many, and it is not un-

143

reasonable to claim that at first many in the Christian church felt that such a critical attitude could be tolerated more readily in respect of the Old Testament than the New. This, if it were true of some, was a misplaced attitude of complacency, for the rigours of historical and literary criticism do not, and cannot, cease at the last page of the Old Testament. Nevertheless such a historical-critical approach is not an end in itself, but merely a means by which some further end can be achieved. To know when the Old Testament literature arose, what were its sources, and what light it brings to bear upon the history of the people from whom it emerged, are simply preliminary tasks towards understanding the life and religion of these people themselves. In many ways this fact was lost sight of by many of the leading scholars of the late nineteenth century who saw the historical enterprise very much as constituting the primary goal. History was elevated to become the queen of the Old Testament sciences. Such scholars shared a conviction that historical truth was of a purer and nobler kind than the truths about the Bible which theologians had previously canvassed. It was more or less assumed to be the fullest meaning of scripture. This is strikingly evident in the work of Wellhausen, who devoted all his considerable energies to the tasks of uncovering the origins of three great world religions: Judaism, Islam and Christianity. We can therefore see a surprising uniformity of motivation underlying his work.

What Wellhausen's *Prolegomena* achieved for Old Testament studies was a better picture of the history of Israel's religious institutions than that which had been afforded by the traditional view which is reflected in the Old Testament itself. It offered a satisfactory working basis from which it became possible to place in a comprehensible sequence the various layers of material containing references to them. That such a sequence made use of a broadly evolutionary theory of development and historical growth is undeniable, but nevertheless it was more credible than the traditional view which it replaced. Since the time of Wellhausen many modifications to this view have been proposed, some of them more necessary and convincing than others. They include some quite radical criticisms of it, which, if upheld, would be tantamount to its rejection. This is in some measure true of the alternative picture of the history of Israel's religion put forward by the Israeli Jewish scholar Y. Kaufmann.[5] In his massive work on the subject this scholar set out a reconstruction of the history of the leading Old Testament institutions of priesthood, temple and sacrifice which adheres more closely to the traditional view, although accepting several basic features of the literary-critical method, and some of the conclusions which Wellhausen had defended. Nonetheless this more radical alternative has not found a wide acceptance beyond the more immediate circle of Kaufmann's pupils, and the mainstream of scholarship has flowed, if at times somewhat sluggishly, along the course dug for it by Wellhausen.

Where the most serious limitations of Wellhausen's scheme become apparent is in his treatment of Israelite religious development as a purely internal, and almost insular, process. Furthermore we can see a false underlying assumption in the way in which he regarded the literary sources as consistent wholes, to be dated close to the time of the latest developments which are to be noted within them. It was this assumption that led Wellhausen to argue that the literary documents of the Pentateuch can be dated quite directly on the evidence of the latest changes in religious practice which is revealed within them. Gunkel saw that this was not necessarily the case, and that these longer literary sources were made up from collections of far older material, so that we can obtain from them a picture in far greater depth of the ongoing religious life of Israel. Markedly too Wellhausen's picture of the development of Israelite religion greatly underestimated the spiritual and moral potentialities present in primitive cultus. Hence certain areas of the Old Testament literature were placed far too late in the scheme of religious and literary development. This is most obvious in the late date ascribed to the composition of the Psalms by Wellhausen's close friend B. Duhm, a point on which Wellhausen himself was wisely more cautious. All the same the resulting picture was somewhat distorted and out of focus, and required to be corrected.

For this we can point most of all to the work of the Norwegian scholar Mowinckel, who had come under the influence, not only of Gunkel, but also of the Danish anthropologist W. Grønbech. In his *Psalmenstudien I–VI* of 1921–24 he endeavoured to show the elaborate nature and religious quality that had belonged to early Israelite cultus, and which has been preserved in written form for us in the Psalter. In this early work of Mowinckel's he reacted too strongly against the prevailing critical viewpoint, so that in turn it is rather onesided. In his later years he did much to improve the situation by his own modification of his earlier views. However, on the question of the importance of the cult for the life and faith of early Israel, and in regard to the argument that the psalms were almost all cultic in their origin, Mowinckel did not retract. He had no need to, for increasingly scholars have come to see that this view is basically sound.

In the years that followed the publication of Mowinckel's *Psalmenstudien* the growing knowledge of the religions of surrounding peoples in the Ancient East served in considerable measure to confirm his view of the cultic nature of early Israelite religion. Surprisingly Mowinckel himself was ill at ease with attempts to use the rediscovered Canaanite materials from Ras Shamra to support his interpretation of the Old Testament psalms. This was in part a reaction against their over-employment in this direction by some other Scandinavian scholars. Although controversies over 'myth and ritual' and 'patternism' have at times beclouded many of the issues involved, it cannot now be questioned that the utmost importance attaches to careful comparisons between Israel's worship and that of its neighbours. What still calls for the most guarded assessments is how this relationship is to be seen and understood. Admittedly in this area an anthropological interest in the presence among geographically separate peoples of similar phenomena has often clashed with a theological concern to defend Israel's uniqueness. Nevertheless the differing aims and methods of each approach have retained a validity within their own spheres. The full extent of the revised picture of early Israelite religion which began to emerge with Mowinckel's work has only slowly obtained adequate recognition.

We can in retrospect see how heavily the late nineteenth century accounts of the history of Israelite religion accepted with extraordinary simplicity the view that religion in general could be understood in terms of a few basic notions such as the fatherhood of God. The study of the structure, organization and aims of worship could be set aside as of little abiding interest. In some respects the transition from presenting a theology of the Old Testament to that of writing a historical study of Israel's religion was undermined by such restricted conceptions of the nature of religion. Important aspects of the subject could easily be overlooked, or dismissed as secondary.

Another factor which has led to a substantially revised presentation of the history of the literature of the Old Testament has been the discovery that didactic writings, comparable to those of Israelite wisdom, can be found outside Israel from as early as the second millennium BC. The discovery of the teaching of Amen-em-ope from Egypt showed that there was no intrinsic reason why some forms of written wisdom should not have appeared in Israel quite early, and certainly before the exile. In a more general way the revisions that the advances of scholarship have rendered necessary in the dates accorded to the psalmody and proverbial teaching of Israel have raised issues which extend beyond the origin of the books of Psalms and Proverbs. In particular they have affected very extensively the picture of prophecy and its background.

From a theological viewpoint it is evident that the progress and achievements of Old Testament criticism have not always produced the kind of results that theologians would regard as most desirable. We have noted that, although a strong religious interest motivated the pioneers of Old Testament criticism, the real focus of their achievement was a search for a fuller understanding of Israel's history. It is not surprising therefore that the historical conclusions reached by this enquiry have seldom been able to solve theological questions. The theological perspective has certainly not been altogether absent, since a large number of scholars engaged in the study of the Old Testament have done so out of a deep religious attachment to it. The history of Israel itself has been interpreted as a history of salvation, and such claims have given rise to a very extensive debate about the nature of history and its relationship to historical research. Without wishing to embark upon this debate at this point, we must nonetheless note that there is an important, and very complex, relationship between events and their interpretation. This is evident enough from the Old Testament itself, which contains a significant interweaving of history and faith, the interrelationships of which cannot be denied and which make it impossible to understand either one without the other.

While we can readily see the limitations imposed upon biblical study by an approach to the Old Testament which has sometimes been almost exclusively preoccupied with history and historical questions, we must also recognize the serious dangers of ignoring them. On the other side it is also unsatisfactory to try to find in the Old Testament a body of timeless doctrines which can be easily and smoothly set apart from the connection with particular people, events and institutions. When we look back we can see that Old Testament scholarship moved dramatically from a concern with a theology of the Old Testament in the early part of the nineteenth century to one which was almost completely taken up with the study of different aspects of Old Testament history—of Israel, its religion and its literature. History exercised a kind of mesmeric power over scholars. Only now is scholarship beginning to become conscious of this sufficiently to try to reach beyond it, and to accord a fuller place to the more directly theological issues.

It is in recognition of this dilemma that B. S. Childs in particular has come to speak of a crisis in biblical theology.[7] In the sense in which the nineteenth century pietists looked for such a theology, it is evident that literary-critical studies have complicated, rather than facilitated, such a task. To seek such a theology is to look for something that the ancient Israelites did not deliberately formulate as such, and one may well question whether it would have been possible for them to do so without the formal basis of the classical philosophical tradition. It is in response to such a difficulty that B. S. Childs has himself endeavoured to bring back into the theological discussion of the text of the Old Testament aspects of its pre-critical interpretation which the historico-critical method of the nineteenth century had bypassed.[8] As a consequence the way in which the New Testament interprets the Old, and the established hermeneutical traditions of both Jews and Christians, have been drawn back into the discussion of the theological meaning of the Old Testament.

In conclusion we may look briefly at the direction in which further research on the Old Testament is headed. That a great deal of further research into a number of literary and religious questions remains to be conducted needs no elaboration. Some areas of the literature still remain very obscure, and nowhere is this more true than in the prophets. The value of a redaction-critical approach has here to be more fully explored. What is overall of even greater importance is the awareness that there can be no going back to seek a return to some kind of theological, or hermeneutical, approach which ignores the demands of proper historical method. The roots of the Old Testament in real history reach down too far for this to be possible, and the vagaries of the older patterns of allegorical and typological interpretation which are to be found in abundance in patristic and mediaeval Christian exegesis can now command no confidence.

While there are today signs of a great deal of fresh theological questioning about the proper scope, and inherent limitations, of historico-critical method, we can nevertheless claim that the century which has passed since the publication of Wellhausen's *Prolegomena* has witnessed sound progress and solid achievements. That there have also been limitations and shortcomings, with the exploration of a number of false trails, need not be denied, since such are inherent in all worthwhile scholarly endeavour. They in no way lessen our respect for the attainments of the past, nor prevent us from trying to build upon these for the future.

The different methods of research that have moulded the major efforts of Old Testament study: literary criticism, form criticism, tradition-history and redaction criticism all show a degree of interdependence which means that no one of them can be upheld without due regard for the others. What we have seen in the development of scholarship has been a constant process of redefining aims and fashioning the methods and tools appropriate to reach them.

Since the majority of those who read the Old Testament do so because of its religious interest and concern, it is natural that the questions relating to its theological meaning should have a particular priority. That in the last two decades so much has been written on the theology of the Old Testament is adequate recognition of this fact. Nevertheless we may expect much from other fields of enquiry also, and continue to look for the science of archaeology to contribute its own share of new evidence and new material. Most of all one may hope that what has thus far been achieved in Old Testament research will continue to interest the minds of men, and speak to their most profound aspirations, that the continuance of the task of interpreting it will remain assured.

---

1. G. Ebeling, 'Was heisst 'Biblische Theologie'?', in *Wort und Glaube*, Tübingen, 1960, pp. 69–89; English translation by J. W. Leitch, 'The Meaning of Biblical Theology', in *Word and Faith*, London, 1963, pp. 79–97.
2. An interesting memoir of Ewald is to be found in T. Witton Davies, *Heinrich Ewald. Orientalist and Theologian, 1803–1903. A Centenary Appreciation*, London, 1903.
3. Cf. F. Boschwitz, *Julius Wellhausen*, pp. 41ff.
4. The phrase is cited by G. von Rad, *Old Testament Theology*, Volume I, p. 107 note 3, from the writings of E. Troeltsch.
5. Y. Kaufmann, see above note 32 to chapter 2.
6. So especially in the essay by R. Bultmann, 'The Significance of the Old Testament for Christian Faith', in *The Old Testament and Christian Faith*, edited by B. W. Anderson, New York, 1969, pp. 8–35.
7. B. S. Childs, *Biblical Theology in Crisis*, Philadelphia, 1970.
8. See especially his *Exodus. A Commentary*, London, 1974.

Index of Authors

152